Forgotten
COLORADO SILVER

Forgotten COLORADO SILVER

Joseph Lesher's Defiant Coins

Robert D. Leonard Jr., Kenneth L. Hallenbeck and Adna G. Wilde, Jr.

THE History PRESS

Published by The History Press
Charleston, SC
www.historypress.net

First published 2017

Manufactured in the United States

ISBN 9781467135252

Library of Congress Control Number: 2017934933

Contents

Acknowledgements

The person most responsible for seeing this new, authoritative account of the Lesher Dollar through to completion is Robert S. Kincaid. He began researching its history in 1984 at the Teller County Courthouse and the Victor Library, and in 1994, he hired genealogist Sandra Slater as research director; she collected information on each person associated with Lesher's project—particularly local issuers John E. Nelson and James Slusher and Arthur B. Bumstead's time in Nebraska—eventually assembling it into a binder. She also hired photographer and researcher Jo Ann Knudson, Salida Museum director Judy Micklich, researcher Donna Nevens, researcher Betty Clifton, researchers John and Carol Fox, researcher Wynona Hennessey and researcher Priscilla Mangnall. Bob prepared files for every aspect of the Lesher Dollar and has been relentless in pursuing an author to present this information. He received encouragement and assistance from John J. Ford Jr., Wayne K. Homren, Q. David Bowers, Edward Rochette, Cripple Creek District Museum director Jan Collins and many others.

The present authors (and others) each considered working on the project at various times in the past, but it remained in limbo until Robert Leonard located a suitable publisher as a result of Bob Kincaid's constant prodding. Sandra Slater has continued to support the Lesher research, always responding promptly to questions.

In addition to those who assisted Bob, thanks are due to collector and Lesher Dollar researcher Christopher Marchase, researcher Dan Owens, researcher and reviewer Tom DeLorey, former ANS curator of North

American Coins and Currency Robert W. Hoge, former ANS assistant curator of American Coins and Currency Matthew Wittman, ANS archivist and Francis D. Campbell librarian David Hill, National Archives archivist Wayne Deceaser, genealogist Betty Voigt, librarian Eunice Borrelli, collector Brad Rodgers and collector Michael Greenspan.

Chapter 1

The Cripple Creek Mining District

In the 1870s, while building a shed over a spring on Levi Welty's ranch in El Paso County, Colorado, one of his sons was struck by a falling log near the stream. Startled, Levi moved suddenly, and his gun discharged, wounding his hand. The gunshot frightened a calf, which jumped into the stream and injured its leg. Afterward, Levi remarked, "That sure is some crippled creek."

So they say. (Variants of this legend exist.) Whatever the origin, the name Cripple Creek stuck and was soon applied to the settlement that sprang up nearby and then to an entire district.

But there would have been no district except for the determination of one man: Bob Womack, "a part-time cowboy and full-time drinker." Grubstaked by a Colorado Springs dentist in 1890, Womack stayed sober long enough to dig a thirty-foot shaft with pick and shovel, searching for the source of an extremely rich ore sample he had discovered eleven years before. And he found it but—due to his reputation—was only able to sell a half interest in his discovery for $500. Though little notice was taken of Womack's strike, other prospectors followed and established many rich mines. But Womack himself died virtually penniless on August 10, 1909.

As of 1900, the Cripple Creek District consisted of the cities of Cripple Creek and Victor, plus the nearby towns of Altman, Arequa, Independence and many others, though it seems to have had no definite boundary. In 1891, gold production barely registered at $499, but it soared to $583,010 the next year and $2,010,367 in 1893. Gold production exceeded $10 million in 1897

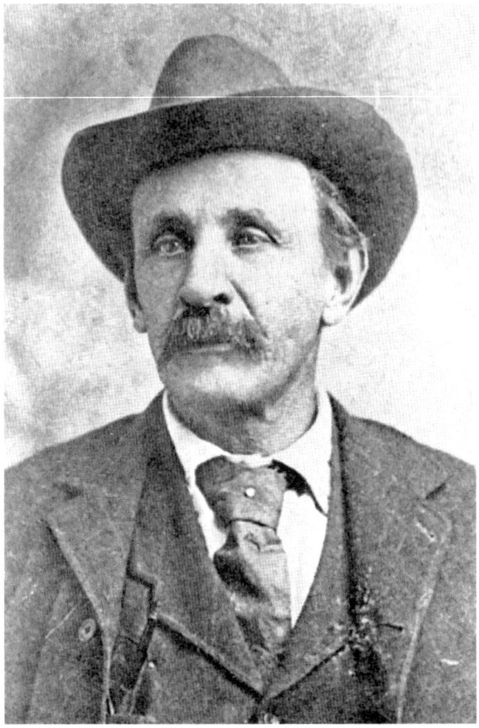

Right: Robert Womack, discoverer of gold at Cripple Creek. *Courtesy of Cripple Creek District Museum.*

Below: Cripple Creek and Victor panorama. *Library of Congress Prints and Photographs Division.*

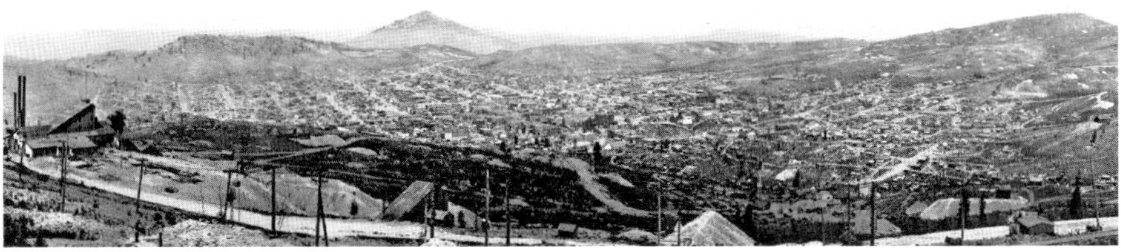

and, in 1899, $15 million. The all-time peak was $18,073,539 in 1900, after which a slow decline began. (Severe labor troubles crimped production in 1894 and 1903–4; see chapter 8.)

Though the principal product was gold, not inconsiderable amounts of silver were also extracted: 82,520 fine ounces in 1899, 80,166 in 1900 and 90,884 in 1901.

This production required the efforts of over 10,000 miners by 1893. Population of the Cripple Creek District grew to 25,000 by 1895, approaching 50,000 by 1900. The chief population centers were Cripple Creek, population 10,147 in 1900, and Victor—where the richest gold mines

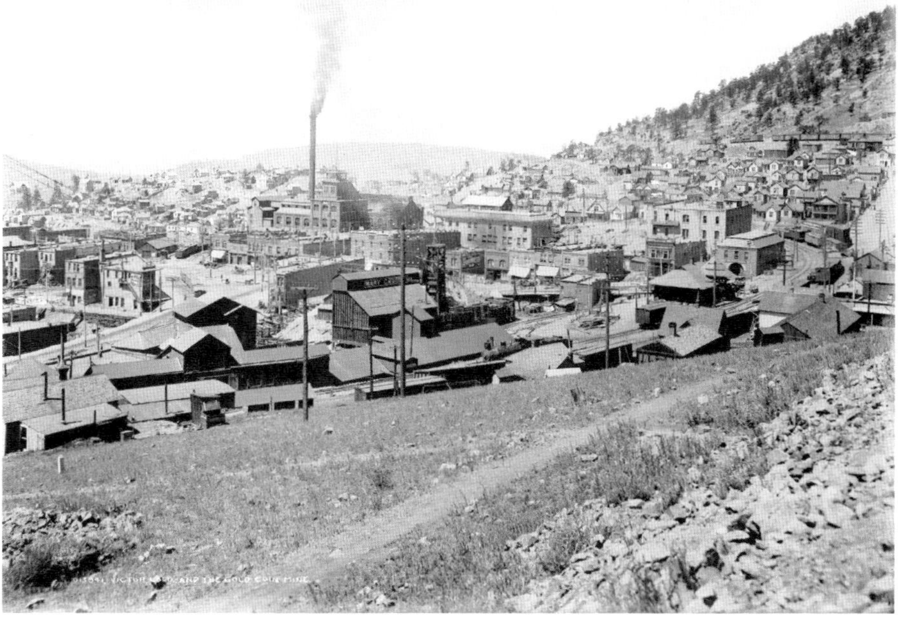

Bird's-eye view, Victor, Colorado. *Wikimedia Commons.*

were—population 1,174. Both Cripple Creek and Victor were spread out over valleys, though the smaller Victor had a more compact business district. Population growth was such that in 1899, the Cripple Creek District, plus a considerable area to the north (but excluding Pikes Peak), was split off from El Paso County; a new county, Teller, was established, with the seat at Cripple Creek.

The Cripple Creek District, indeed the whole state of Colorado, was heavily Democratic then. In the 1900 presidential election, Teller County voted Democratic better than two to one; Democrat William Jennings Bryan carried the state by a plurality of nearly thirty thousand votes. And when Theodore Roosevelt visited Victor that fall while campaigning for vice president on the Republican ticket, he was prevented from speaking by local miners, and his party was actually stoned.

Chapter 2

Private Coins and Free Silver

The Constitution provides that "No State shall...coin money...[or] make any thing but gold and silver coin a tender in payment of debts" (Article I, Section 10). Why the latter is no longer true is a subject for another book, but a hint will be found in chapter 8.

Since the Constitution also gives Congress the power to coin money and regulate the value thereof (Article I, Section 8), one would naturally think that the federal government had a monopoly on all minting. But this assumption was tested in 1830 by Templeton Reid, an immigrant gunsmith and clockmaker in Milledgeville, Georgia. Gold had been discovered in the Cherokee Nation in 1828, and thousands of "twenty-niners" converged on north Georgia the next year. At first, huge amounts were taken out: in Gilmer County, Zeke Spriggs stuffed so much gold dust in his pockets from a single day's panning that his suspenders snapped. Most of the gold was illegally taken from lands of the Cherokee Nation; Georgia then annexed their territory in 1830 and expelled them.

Conveying all this gold to the mint in Philadelphia was problematic: it took a long time, and there was the risk of robbers. So Reid set up his own mint, coining $2½, $5 and $10 gold pieces. It soon failed, but not because it was unconstitutional (the Constitution forbade *states* to coin money but omitted any mention of *persons*); rather, some of these coins turned out to be worth significantly less than face value. This precedent being established, other private mints were founded in Rutherfordton, North Carolina, 1831; Salt Lake City, 1848; Oregon City, Oregon, 1849;

San Francisco, 1849–54; Denver, Jefferson Territory (unofficial)/Kansas Territory, 1860; Tarryall Mines, Colorado, 1861; and Georgia Gulch, Colorado, 1861.

But in 1861, the Civil War broke out, and soon gold and then silver coins vanished from circulation. Many millions of anonymous copper cents ("patriotic Civil War tokens") were issued by manufacturers from Boston to Chicago. Realizing that this vast outpouring was actually legal, Congress prohibited the issue of one- and two-cent tokens on April 22, 1864, and followed up on June 8 with an act abolishing private coinage of any kind: "any coins of gold or silver or other metals or alloys of metals, intended for the use and purpose of the United States or of foreign countries, or of original design…"

Since then, the only exceptions permitted have been tokens good at a single issuer, with a value stated or implied (drink, bus fare, bridge toll, parking, videogame play, etc.). Obviously, minting private coins under such restrictions would be quite a challenge, and even if done, would anyone want them?

In time, the answer was *yes*. After France agreed to pay an indemnity of 5 billion francs to Germany in 1871, Germany adopted the gold standard, and the following year, it was joined by Sweden, Norway and Denmark. Millions of dollars of demonetized German silver coins were sold as bullion between 1873 and 1879. In 1873, the United States eliminated the silver dollar as currency, but because none were in circulation (greenback dollars remained below par until 1879), no notice was taken at the time of the "Crime of 1873," as it was later called by Western mining interests. The same decade saw silver production from the Comstock Lode rising, peaking in 1877.

These and other factors (including the Panic of 1873 and the Great Railroad Strike of 1877) combined to suppress the price of newly mined silver, and it fell from $1.322 per ounce (in greenbacks) in 1872 to $1.278 (in greenbacks) in 1874 and to $1.123 (in gold) in 1879. This decline led Western silver interests to demand price supports, and in this they were aided by those wishing to inflate the money supply (farmers, debtors) by the unlimited minting of silver into dollars ("Free Coinage of Silver").

Their efforts resulted in the Bland-Allison Act of 1878, which became law over President Hayes's veto. It called for the Treasury to purchase not less than $2 million of silver every month and coin it into silver dollars. It was assumed that these dollars would go into circulation, but between 1878 and 1888, nearly 300 million silver dollars were minted, but only 50 million

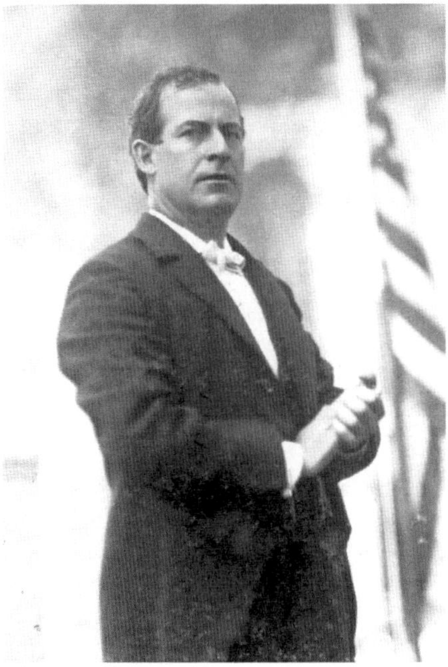

William Jennings Bryan as candidate for president, 1896.

left the Treasury. (The balance were held as reserves for paper silver certificates, which did circulate.)

But the price of silver continued dropping, to only $0.935 in 1889. So in 1890, the Sherman Silver Purchase Act was adopted. It called for the Treasury to buy 4.5 million ounces of silver every month (99 percent of 1890's domestic production!), and these new coins and notes were redeemable in gold. While this had the desired effect of boosting silver prices—to $1.046 in 1890, $0.988 in 1891, but only $0.871 in 1892—it led to silver displacing gold as currency to the point that the nation's gold reserve fell below $100,000,000 by June 1893—the minimum thought necessary to defend the paper money. By this time, the country was in the grip of the Panic of 1893.

President Grover Cleveland called a special session of Congress to repeal the Sherman Act, and it was repealed on November 1, 1893. At once, the price of silver collapsed, dropping to $0.635 in 1894 and $0.602 in 1899.

By 1896, however, Cleveland was so unpopular with rank-and-file Democrats that the Democratic National Convention, in an unprecedented step, rejected a resolution commending an administration of its own party. It turned instead to the charismatic William Jennings Bryan, a fierce advocate of Free Silver. But he was defeated, and when nominated again in 1900, he lost by an even larger plurality. Free Silver supporters had been thwarted.

Chapter 3

Joseph Lesher

Pioneer, Promoter and Minter

One of the best-known men in the Cripple Creek Mining District was Free Silver advocate Joseph Lesher. Born on July 12, 1838, on a farm in Ohio, one of eleven children, he was descended from German pioneers who settled in Pennsylvania before the Revolutionary War. As an adult, he stood five feet nine inches tall and had blue eyes, light hair and a "fair" complexion.

In 1860, he left the family farm, then in Wood County, Ohio, to become a "merchant." Then came the Civil War and the Enrollment Act of 1863: all able-bodied male citizens and foreigners intending to become citizens between the ages of twenty and forty-five were required to register for military duty. The first draftees were called up on July 11. Joseph Lesher registered for the draft in Wood County by the July 1 deadline. He is clearly shown as "married"—though he wasn't then (a clerical error? or an attempt to evade service?). But he was not selected.

Not even a year later, on May 2, 1864, he enlisted in the Ohio National Guard as a corporal (Company K, Ohio 144th Infantry Regiment) for a one-hundred-day stint, along with his younger brother Aaron. (The governors of Ohio, Indiana, Illinois, Iowa and Wisconsin offered to raise a force of volunteers to serve for one hundred days, to be outfitted and paid by the United States. These troops were to support the campaign of 1864 by relieving a large number of battle-hardened veterans from garrison and guard duty, allowing them to participate in the campaign.)

But instead of easy duty, Lesher's unit was attacked by Mosby's Rangers while leisurely guarding a six-hundred-unit wagon train; five men were killed and another six wounded. Sixty were captured, of whom twenty-eight died in the Confederate prison in Salisbury, North Carolina, and four others elsewhere. Only Lesher, his brother and "three or four others" escaped, he told his wife years later (somewhat exaggerated, typical for war stories).

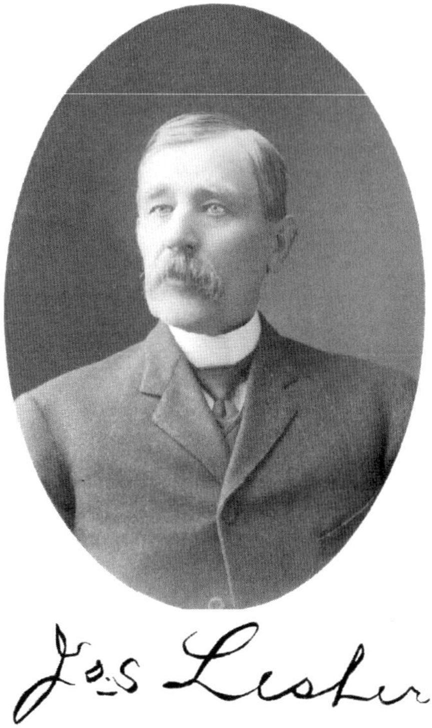

Joseph Lesher, circa 1907. *Courtesy of American Numismatic Society, New York.*

Less than three weeks later, on August 31, he was mustered out at Camp Chase, in Columbus, Ohio. After leaving the army, "he was engaged in the mercantile business, but, tiring of this, he decided to go to Colorado," Mrs. Lesher wrote in 1921. He apparently had another motive for leaving Ohio, however; at least five Wood County creditors filed attachments on his property after his departure.

Lesher set out in May 1865. His wife continued, "He crossed the plains behind a yoke of oxen, without encountering any Indians, though they had been troublesome that year and killed a number of travelers." On August 20, he arrived in Central City, Gilpin County, Colorado. There he learned of the Belmont Lode, discovered the previous summer in what soon became Georgetown, Colorado, and moved there in 1866.

"On arriving at Georgetown he went to work as a miner, and was the first man to use a 'Burley' [Burleigh] drill in Colorado," Mrs. Lesher wrote. This drill, invented by Fitchburg, Massachusetts machinist Charles Burleigh in 1866, was the first reliable percussive rock drill. Beginning in 1868, Burleigh took a personal interest in Georgetown mining: on Sherman Mountain, Clear Creek County, the Burleigh Tunnel was constructed to intersect several deep lodes and was still being enlarged as late as March 1870.

When the census taker found Joseph Lesher on July 28, 1870, he was still toiling as a miner in the Georgetown area, Clear Creek County. However, about this time he began to be "engaged in the mining business for himself, and was very successful," according to his wife. (Her recollections of what Lesher told her appear to compress his actual activities there.) In any case, he seems to have begun prospecting himself.

In 1872, Lesher's father died in Wood County, Ohio. That November, Lesher returned to Ohio and founded a livery and sale stable in Toledo, in partnership with Warren S. Waite. They missed the deadline for the *1872–3 Toledo City Directory* but are listed in every directory from *1873–4* through *1878–79*. In 1878, he bought out his partner and continued running the business himself until 1883.

He then moved back south to Wood County and turned to "farming in the vicinity," he told Lesher Dollar researcher Farran Zerbe in 1914. After a few years, however, he began making extended trips to Colorado, though maintaining residence in Ohio. Zerbe understood that Lesher had moved back to Colorado as early as 1886, and Lesher gave dates of 1888 and 1889 in pension applications of 1904 and 1907. But he applied for an "Invalid"

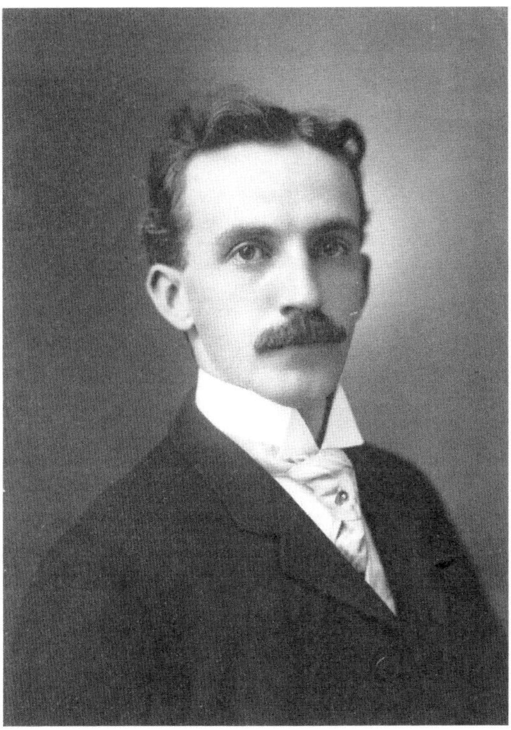

Farran Zerbe, 1910. *Courtesy of American Numismatic Society Archives.*

Civil War pension on May 7, 1888, from Perry City, Wood County (it was refused on the grounds that he had "no evidence of disability" when mustered out), and on July 17, 1890, he married Miss Abby Jane (Jennie) Cole, forty, in Waterville, Wood County.

About seven months later, in February 1891, Lesher visited Pueblo, Colorado, "endeavoring to form a company to construct and operate a smelting furnace of which he is the inventor," according to the *Denver News* of February 20, 1891, copying the *Pueblo Review*. He gave his address as Toledo, Ohio. Lesher's invention consisted of a blast furnace fired by natural gas, constructed so as to keep the charge molten long enough for it to be run off into ingots externally.

Lesher later boasted of living in Georgetown, Central City, Leadville (but he is not listed in any Leadville city directory from 1886 through 1894), and the Silver San Juan (Silverton, Colorado) and stated in a 1908 pension application that he resided in Aspen, Colorado, from 1887 to 1892. During this time, he acquired a silver mine near Central City that was profitable prior to the price slump of 1892.

In 1892, the Leshers left Ohio for good to move to the booming Cripple Creek Mining District. In the spring of 1893, he opened an ice cream stand in Mound City, between Cripple Creek and Victor. But he seems to have made most of his fortune from dealing in Victor real estate; transactions of the Leshers have been noted as early as September 7, 1894, in the records of El Paso County (prior records are illegible). Lesher listed his occupation as "Real Estate" in the *1896 Victor City Directory*. In the 1897 directory, Lesher added mining to his listing, and in the 1900 directory, he dropped real estate. By November 13, 1900, the *Victor Daily Record* described him as "one of the monied men of the camp."

Lesher put these funds to good use with his Referendum Dollar scheme (chapter 4), which occupied much of his time from 1900 through 1903. Curiously, he was listed as a gold miner in the census of 1900, but perhaps the enumerator confused min*ing* with min*er*. Even while promoting his Referendum Dollars, Lesher was actively involved with mining properties, selling a two-thirds interest in his lease of the Addie C. claim for a "large" sum on April 10, 1902, and (with partners) the Jessie lode outright on November 29, 1902.

By 1904, however, his financial situation had deteriorated. He revived his application for an "Invalid" pension, claiming the same infirmities as in 1888 and adding "eyesight much impared [*sic*] by age"; he was sixty-five. He stated that his occupation was "Quartz-mining when able." On October 24, he was awarded an invalid pension of a paltry eight dollars per month, on grounds of senile disability and various other ailments.

The *1905 Victor City Directory* actually listed his occupation as "miner," which, if true, shows a dramatic drop in his financial status. On May 9, 1905, he applied for an increase in his invalid pension, alleging additional infirmities, and was granted an increase to $10 per month. Later that year, he sold a quit-claim deed for a city lot in Victor for $100.

In the spring of 1906, he moved to Hercules, Churchill County, Nevada, to prospect for silver, retaining his house in Victor. The *Rocky Mountain News* of May 26, 1906, reported that he sent six samples of ore from the Fairview district in Churchill County, Nevada, to Victor assayer John Vincent, which returned up to five thousand ounces of silver to the ton. But Lesher seems to have been unable to capitalize on this strike.

Following the Act of February 6, 1907, Lesher applied for another increase in his pension and was awarded a raise to $12. The following year, he sold—with two partners—a mining deed for two properties in the Cripple Creek Mining District for $1,000.

When he turned seventy in 1908, he applied for a further pension increase. He was then living in Rawhide, Esmeralda County, Nevada, having moved there from Wonder, Nevada (founded May 1906). He received another increase, to fifteen dollars. Shortly thereafter, he returned to Victor. The census of 1910 listed him as dealing in real estate on his own account, and the *1912 Victor City Directory* listed his occupation as "Real Estate & Mining."

On August 11, 1913, Lesher requested yet another increase in his pension, on "account of age." The Bureau of Pensions requested proof that he was really seventy-five years old but was eventually satisfied, and his pension advanced to twenty-one dollars per month. That same year, he took an interest in the Big Four gold- and silver-mining property in Larimer County, Colorado, working a claim there briefly with his brother Aaron.

The following March, he was back in the Big Four property. The *Rocky Mountain News* of April 2, 1914, citing the *Montezuma Journal*, wrote:

> *Joseph Lesher of Victor, who has been interested in that oil venture, also had his eyes open for indications of uranium in that vicinity, with the result that after some time prospecting he struck the present body of ore. Early this week he went down to the mine with three Telluride men who desire to lease this property and work it this season....It looked like it would pay to prospect for this valuable ore, and it seems that Lesher has started this work.*

(These strange juxtapositions show Lesher, on the one hand, claiming in 1913 an "Invalid" pension on the grounds that he is "wholly" unable to support himself because he is "all most blind catarack coming on both eyes and bad case of rupture," while the next year finds him clambering over rocks in northern Colorado at age seventy-five prospecting for uranium! Mrs. Lesher told Farran Zerbe in a 1934 letter that "no one took him to be over 65 years old. His hair was not grey.")

But by 1914, he really was in difficulty. His capital was much diminished, and he was unable to exploit his prospecting discoveries fully. In fact, his wife wrote to the Bureau of Pensions in March 1918 that "he has not money in hand to pay his funeral expenses."

In January 1918, Joseph Lesher became sick. He had a very bad cough, which improved in a few days after seeing a doctor, but then he developed dropsy. He lived only another six months. Ten days before his death, his pension was increased one last time, to thirty dollars a month. On July 4, at 8:00 a.m., he succumbed to "chronic cardiac dilitation [*sic*, enlarged heart], eight days before his eightieth birthday. He was buried on July 7, 1918, in Sunnyside Cemetery, Victor, Colorado. Mrs. Lesher lived in the same house in Victor until June 15, 1938, and rests beside him in Sunnyside.

Joseph Lesher was recalled in the *Cripple Creek Times* and *Victor Record* as a GAR veteran and the originator of an octagonal silver dollar, though the reporter was confused as to the date of issue. In her letter of March 28, 1918, Mrs. Lesher complained that, though her husband had great ideas in oil, mining "and several other things," he lacked "having risk capital to carry it through and the other fellow would make the money."

She might have added that he was a great promoter: he made sure that his Toledo livery stable was listed in the city directory in boldface type every year (except for 1882, when he apparently missed the deadline). But he outdid himself in publicizing his Referendum Dollars, giving expansive interviews and issuing an impressive advertising card. He had the optimism of a prospector, always expecting to make his fortune from his current project.

Still, Joseph Lesher would be little known today but for his one great success: he minted his own coins and put them into circulation, notwithstanding the Act of June 8, 1864. He decided that if the Treasury wouldn't buy any more silver to coin into dollars, then *he* would. "One day while talking with some businessmen he remarked that he thought he could make something that would be accepted as money. They did not agree with him, but soon afterwards he produced his first Lesher Referendum Coin," Mrs. Lesher wrote in 1921. And even the U.S. Secret Service couldn't stop him.

Chapter 4

The Lesher "Referendum" Dollar

Colorado was devastated by the huge drop in the price of silver caused by repeal of the Sherman Act. In 1893, Governor Davis Waite was the first to suggest some sort of private minting: he proposed that Colorado should use its sovereign powers to buy the silver mined in the state and send it to Mexico to be coined into dollars, which would then be returned to Colorado and placed in circulation. This ridiculous scheme—his opponents lampooned it as "fandango dollars"—was practically laughed out of the legislature, though Colorado senator E.O. Wolcott is said to have entertained it also.

But then Joseph Lesher came along and actually produced Colorado coins. In 1900, apparently, he wrote to Colorado senator Henry M. Teller for an opinion as to the legality of his proposed project, receiving assurances "that so long as he did not imitate the lawful money of the United States he would meet with no interference upon the part of the federal authorities," per the *Denver Post* of November 12, 1900. (This was bad advice, as we shall see, for the Act of June 8, 1864—later codified in the Revised Statutes of the United States as Section 5461—forbade private coinage of any kind, including pieces "of original design.")

Thus encouraged, Lesher set about designing his coins, taking several steps to disguise their true nature: he made them octagonal instead of round; omitted any design, using inscriptions only; called each piece a "souvenir" and "a commodity"; called the face value a "price" (but fatally used "face value" on the reverse); and deliberately misspelled "currency" as "curency," apparently in the hope that he could argue that "curency" and "currency" were two different things. Finally, he labeled each one a "Referendum," indicating that they were referred to the people for acceptance or rejection.

One puzzling decision was to make the face value $1.25 instead of an even dollar. Lesher's thinking was "that silver should be sold for $1.29 an ounce, and that to sell an ounce for less than $1.25 would be conniving at its depreciation," he told a reporter for the *Denver Post*. But to make the face value the full $1.29 would raise difficulties in making change.

That fall, Lesher traveled to Denver to have them struck. He selected a metal stamping company, probably the Denver Novelty Works, and it assigned Frank F. Hurd, a manufacturing jeweler, to make the dies. (In his 1901 "Referendum" trademark application, Lesher said that he had been using this trademark since October 5, 1900, perhaps the day he delivered the designs to Hurd.) He then purchased silver bullion "from the smelters" and placed an initial order for one hundred pieces, serially numbered, to test the market.

In about a month, his "Referendums" were ready, and Lesher returned to Denver to pick them up. On the morning of November 12, 1900, back in Victor, he announced his scheme to the world. The morning *Victor Daily Record* of November 13, 1900, was blown away:

> *VICTOR MAN STARTS A MINT*
> *The Unique Enterprise of an Ex-Miner Who*
> *Still Has Faith in Silver*
> *The Coins From His Mint Contain Just One*
> *Ounce Of Pure Silver But Are Worth*
> *$1.25 Apiece Because Redeemable in*
> *United States Money—A Scheme*
> *To Open Idle Mines*
>
> *The enterprise of Victor citizens is proverbial, and whether they undertake to set the fashion, in the reception of political spell binders* [an allusion to the stoning of Theodore Roosevelt; see chapter 1] *or break the record in gold production, they are pretty likely to succeed.*
>
> *They believe that Victor should have everything any other city has. Denver has a mint* [actually it was merely a government assay office then and did not become a mint until 1906], *so a Victor man has established a mint also. The Victor mint will coin nothing but silver dollars and the dollars will be worth 25 cents more than the Denver*

product [they were then coined at Philadelphia, New Orleans and San Francisco, but not Denver].

The proprietor of the new mint is Joseph Lesher, one of the pioneers of Colorado. For 20 years he has lived and labored in the silver camps of the state. Georgetown, Central [City], *Leadville and "Silver San Juan" have known him. When silver declined and gold was found south of Pike's peak* [sic] *he came to Victor and prospered. Fortunate investments in real estate multiplied his small capital and at this writing he is one of the monied men of the camp.*

Mr. Lesher has faith in silver. He also has a sincere desire for its enlarged use. This desire is not entirely unselfish, for Mr. Lesher owns a silver mine near Central [City] *that was worked at a profit before the slump in '92, but has since been idle.*

For years Mr. Lesher has believed that it would be possible as well as beneficial for Colorado to coin its depreciated silver and use it to facilitate exchange and so promote business....

First he had a die manufactured in Denver. Then he purchased silver bullion from the smelters. The metal was next rolled out in thin sheets and cut by the die into sexagonal [sic] *pieces, each containing exactly one ounce of pure silver* [sic; the Lesher Dollar actually reads "coin" silver].

Before installing his mint, Mr. Lesher applied to Senator Teller for information and was advised that there would be no legal objection to his enterprise if he refrained from imitating government money. This he has carefully done and his coins differ so greatly both in shape and inscription from legal tender that a blind man can not be deceived by them.

With his present facilities the money-maker can turn out 100 dollars a day. The silver costs at present quotations about 65 cents an ounce and the expense of coining is about 15 cents, so the Lesher "referendum" dollar represents an outlay of 80 cents. The manufacturer charges $1.25 for one of them.

He calls them "referendum" dollars because no one is compelled to take them against his will. In other words, they are referred to the people for acceptance or rejection. Although Mr. Lesher is convinced that the intrinsic value of an ounce of silver is $1.29, he does not insist that everyone shall accept his valuation and is prepared to guarantee the parity of his dollars by redeeming each coin in lawful money of the United States. He keeps his cash at the Bank of Victor and expects to arrange with the cashier to cash the "referendum" dollars in the same manner that checks are cashed.

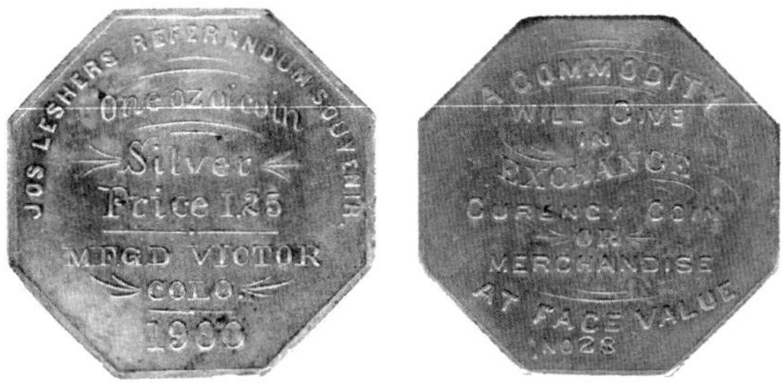

Actual size, 35 mm. *Courtesy of Christopher Marchase.*

> *The coins are a little thicker and much heavier than the United States dollars, but no greater in circumference. They are quite handsome in appearance. On one side is the inscription: "Joseph Lesher's Referendum Souvenir. one ounce of coin silver. Price $1.25. Mf'd Victor, Colo., 1900" and on the other "A Commodity. Will give in exchange currency, coin or merchandise at face value. No—."* [sic]
>
> *Each coin is numbered consecutively.*
>
> *Mr. Lesher believes that the merchants of Colorado could put his souvenirs into circulation by accepting them for goods and using them to pay clerks, rent and local expenses. The silver mine owners could pay off their miners in referendum dollars and so open many idle properties.*
>
> *The mint has turned out 100 of the coins, but no effort has been made to put them into circulation. The manufacturer will first sell them as souvenirs and at the same time try to induce the business men to adopt his scheme....*
>
> *The proprietor is well known to Victor people and all of them will wish him success in his patriotic enterprise.*

Similar stories were carried by other Colorado papers. The November 12 issue of the *Denver Post* added that "Mr. Lesher proposes to demonstrate that the 'intrinsic value' theory is a delusion and a snare," mentioning his cost of production, with the silver cost just over half face value. It said that his promise to redeem his "referendum dollar(s)" at par is safe, because "HE HAS MONEY. As he has a balance of several thousand dollars on deposit at the Bank of Victor, his promise is good for a time at least." This article is illustrated with a facsimile of coin No. 33 (whereabouts unknown today).

Despite the statement that they were made of "coin" silver (.900 fine), Lesher told Farran Zerbe that they were actually about .950 fine.

Lesher was unprepared for the overwhelming response that followed. It "brought novelty seekers in great numbers to Mr. Lesher's house," according to the *Victor Daily Record* of November 14:

> *He and his wife had hardly begun breakfast in their little home when the rush began. It seemed that everyone in town was anxious to become the possessor of a "referendum dollar."... Visitor after visitor was turned away with the assurance that there were not enough dollars on hand to go around.*
>
> *The most welcome visitor of the morning was A.B. Bumstead* [see chapter 7], *proprietor of the grocery on North Third street.... He proposed to accept the souvenirs in exchange for groceries and give them out to anyone who wanted them in change.*
>
> *This took a load off Mr. Lesher's mind, because he did not relish the idea of having his peaceful home turned into a sub-treasury. He gave Mr. Bumstead all the "referendums" he had on hand, about 100, and afterwards referred all customers to the dealer in groceries.*

The *Colorado Springs Gazette* reported the same day that "A.B. Bumstead, a local grocer has secured an option on the output of Lesher's mint for the next five days." Lesher told their reporter that he had orders for five hundred more "and states that his mint has a capacity of 100 a day."

Not mentioned in the *Daily Record* or *Gazette* stories is an item picked up by the reporter for the Denver *Rocky Mountain News* on November 13 that Lesher intended to have a new die made, naming Bumstead: "As soon as...Lesher's corrected die has been made, which will be in a few days, he will issue 500 more coins." At this time, the stock of coins was said to be "exhausted."

As for circulation, the *Daily Record* story of November 15 reported that all of the 100 "souvenirs" were sold "before evening," and "a great many of them were mailed by the purchasers to friends in the East." None of the new coins returned to the till, Bumstead said. "The next of five hundred Souvenirs will be ready for market next Friday [November 21]." The November 16 *Denver Post* echoed this and added that Lesher "has applied to the government for a copyright on the inscription and form of his souvenirs," as a protection against imitators. (He meant a trademark, not a copyright, and in fact he did not get around to starting the paperwork until January 25, 1901.)

Meanwhile, Hurd was becoming uneasy about his role in the Referendum Dollar craze after reading some of the press accounts. On the morning of November 17, he called on Secret Service special operative Charles LaSalle at his Denver office, producing a sample and asking for an opinion as to its legality, "as Lesher wanted to make more of the coins." LaSalle and Hurd then went to Assistant U.S. Attorney T.E. McClelland, who said that in his opinion, no law was violated. Hurd promised to have Lesher send a sample Referendum Dollar for review.

On November 19, however, LaSalle received a message from the chief of the Secret Service, ordering him to proceed to Victor, show Lesher Section 5461 and demand surrender of the dies. LaSalle revisited McClelland, who changed his mind. But it was not necessary for LaSalle to travel to distant Victor, for he knew that the dies were right in Denver at Hurd's shop. Upon arriving, he discovered that Lesher himself had just left but would be right back. When Lesher returned, LaSalle asked to see the dies, "and when he showed them," Lesher recalled in 1913, "[LaSalle] drew a small sack out of his pocket and dropped the dies into the sack, and told him he had better quit the business. This was the last he ever saw of those dies."

Lesher accompanied LaSalle to the office of the U.S. Attorney, where the import of Section 5461 was explained to him. "Mr. Lesher said he had no intention to violate the law, and that he was ignorant of the fact that he was doing so, and said he would at once abandon the scheme," per LaSalle's report for November 19.

But Lesher was not so easily cowed as this. The *Victor Daily Record* of November 23 reported that, while in Denver, "he laid the matter before the U.S. District Attorney and that functionary assured him that he could make 'referendum souvenirs' until the silver mines are exhausted without coming in conflict with any existing statute." This contradicts LaSalle's report, so Lesher presumably had a second meeting with McClelland, who advised him on what changes to make in the inscriptions. Lesher ordered new dies, omitting "currency" and "coin" and stating that they could be exchanged for "merchandise" at only a single location, A.B. Bumstead's grocery.

Instead of Hurd, however, Lesher turned to the talented Herman Otto—a German hand engraver who had come to Colorado from London for his health—to make his new dies. Though Otto had worked on the award medals for the 1896 Olympics in Athens and designed a seal for the city of Denver, Lesher gave him little opportunity to use his judgment to best effect,

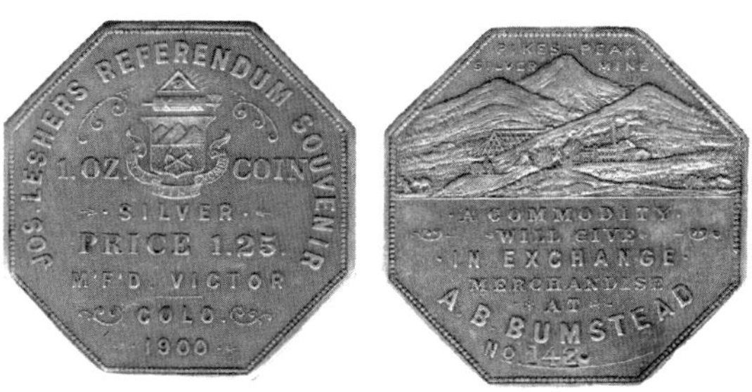

First type—scrolls flank Colorado state arms. Actual size, 35 mm. *Courtesy of Christopher Marchase.*

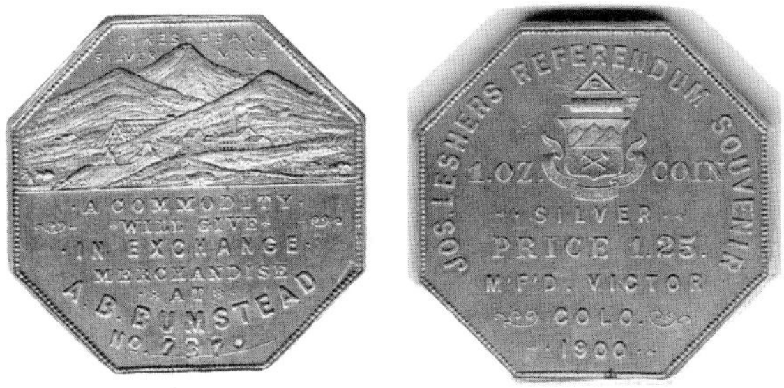

Second type—scrolls omitted. Actual size, 35 mm. *Courtesy of Christopher Marchase.*

dictating the details of the designs. (Sadly, in 1935, Herman Otto, his health failing, committed suicide in a Denver park by shooting himself in the chest.)

The new design was very attractive, showing a scene described as "PIKES—PEAK SILVER MINE," but this was obvious artistic license—there were no mines on Pikes Peak, and those in the Cripple Creek Mining District produced gold almost exclusively. Zerbe stated that these dies cost Lesher sixty dollars a set, equal to a cost of six cents per thousand pieces, which would cut significantly into Lesher's profits.

Lesher then ordered five hundred pieces from the Denver Novelty Works, according to the *Victor Daily News* of November 21. While waiting for them to come in, Bumstead accepted some orders on a "when issued" basis. He reported that only three Lesher Dollars had been presented for redemption, and "[t]hey were not in the store five minutes because other people were just waiting for a chance to buy them."

Though newspaper stories appeared on November 22 and 23 that Lesher had closed his private mint, the *Victor Daily Record* reported on November 23 that he planned to order ten thousand more from the new dies, at a cost of $8,000, returning to Denver to do so the previous day.

Bumstead was still fielding "50 calls a day" when he received a letter from Lesher in Denver on December 1, stating that the engraver was "working night and day" on the dies and that he hoped to return on December 3 with a "trunkful." But Lesher was further delayed by the breakage of the reverse die; a replacement was quickly made, but in the haste to fulfill the order, the scrolls on either side of the state arms were omitted, creating a second variety. This die still exists and is now in the collection of the American Numismatic Society (ANS), New York.

Lesher finally returned to Victor on December 8, bringing back one thousand pieces, "and within five hours he had disposed of 800 of them in the district," reported the *Daily Record*; one of the variety with scrolls was

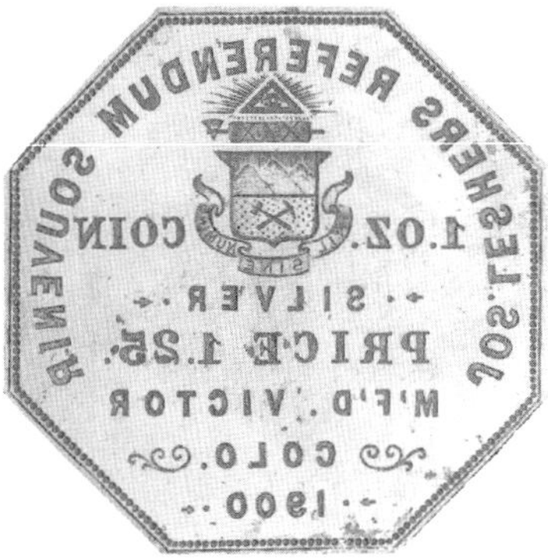

Reverse die for second type of Lesher Dollar (no scrolls). *Courtesy of American Numismatic Society, New York.*

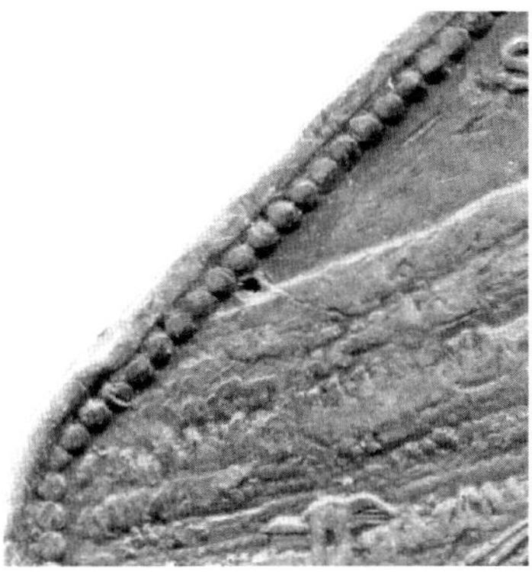

Courtesy of Robert D. Leonard Jr.

illustrated. (Apparently Lesher doubled his initial order of five hundred, but ten thousand was simply a hope. Adna Wilde doubted the stated quantity; see chapter 5 for a reconciliation.) Lesher also mentioned that he planned to transfer production to Chicago to save time and money, but this was never done. This production of one thousand may be the last of the 1900 issues, though the recorded numbers suggest that a second order was probably placed.

To protect himself against unauthorized restrikes, Lesher placed a secret mark on the obverse in the form of a punch where the mining scene joins the left rim. Over 90 percent have this mark.

The Secret Service wasted no time in investigating Lesher's new issue: on December 10, Denver operative Joseph A. Walker wrote to his friend T. Reed Woodbridge, superintendent of the Taylor and Brunton Sampling Works at Victor, enclosing a newspaper clipping and requesting that he buy one and send it to him, promising reimbursement. Special operative LaSalle visited Hurd's shop the same day, only to learn that Hurd was out and Lesher had not come by since the day his dies were seized. The "lady in charge" told LaSalle "that Lesher returned to their place of business the same day the dies were taken from him and said he would succeed in that thing yet; that he said he did not intend to violate the law, but he would find a way to get around it."

And he did. Walker met with United States attorney Greeley W. Whitford on the morning of December 14 and was told "that if the coins were payable in merchandise only, it would make much difference in the prosecution of the case," mentioning a ruling allowing the manufacture of octagonal Indian head one-quarter dollar California gold pieces, which did "not purport to be an imitation, or in substitution of any coin known to the law" (*United States v. Bogart*, 9 Ben. 314, a ruling under Section 5461).

Whitford requested that the Secret Service wait until he could see one of the coins, then "advise [Walker] what evidence he would need to prosecute the case. He said the case would be an important one and probably a test case, as some lawyer had evidently advised Lesher to go ahead and that we could not in any way reach him. [Lesher had no lawyer.] We have determined that when things are in shape that we shall include the lawyer on a charge of conspiracy."

By then Mr. Woodbridge had been heard from, and he reported "that these coins as fast as received are taken up at once as souvenirs and are not yet in circulation as coins," so evidence of circulation was lacking. "There will be no difficulty in proving that Joseph Lesher intended and now intends that these coins shall be circulated as current money," Walker wrote, "as he is a crank on the silver question, and is willing to spend several thousand dollars to carry out his purpose."(!)

On December 14, Walker received Bumstead Dollar No. 160 in the mail, which he transmitted to John E. Wilkie, chief, U.S. Secret Service, the same day (later destroyed). Walker returned to Whitford's office with it and reported, "After a careful examination thereof and of the wording thereon, he said that he did not see that it was issued in violation of Section 5461, U.S.R.S. as interpreted by the decision in *U.S. vs. Bogart*; but will be very glad to prosecute Joseph Lesher if you decide to have [Whitford] do so."

Walker continued, "At present the coins are being taken up as souvenirs, and I am satisfied that they are not circulating as coins, nor being used to buy merchandise with. If it should appear that these coins are being redeemed by the bank at Victor, where Lesher has his account, and charged to Lesher's account, as orders or checks would be charged on presentation, then it seems to me that a 2¢ revenue stamp would be required each time when presented."

Later in the day, LaSalle came by the office to report on his conversation with engraver Frank Hurd. Hurd told him that "he, Hurd, had lately been to Victor, Colorado, and observed the fact that these coins were being used at Bumstead's grocery store as current money," mentioning a rumor that Lesher was "preparing to send a large consignment of these referendum dollars to Chicago in the near future."

However, the Secret Service took no further action against Lesher. Encouraged, he announced later that month that he wished to establish his mint in Denver "if the federal government will allow him to coin his octagonal money." He consulted Whitford and expected to hear from Treasury secretary Lyman Gage.

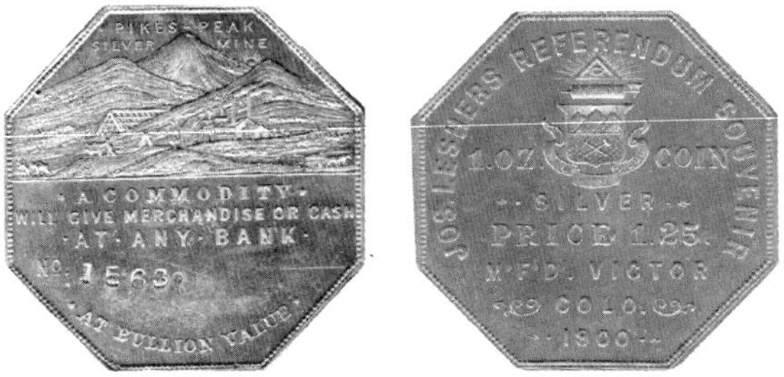

Actual size, 35 mm. *Courtesy of Christopher Marchase.*

Perhaps in anticipation of a successful outcome, Lesher ordered another obverse die, which stated that it was good for "MERCHANDISE OR CASH" "AT • ANY • BANK" "AT BULLION VALUE." Zerbe dryly remarked, "It has not been learned what kind of 'merchandise' banks were expected to give."

The number struck is unknown, but ten specimens are currently recorded, of widely varying numbers; perhaps a run of several hundred was made but most of them melted when Lesher found that it would not pass legal muster. The reverse die is now in the ANS.

On January 25, 1901, Lesher began the process of applying for a trademark for "Referendum" in a curved line; it was registered on April 9. While waiting, he ordered a die reading "TRADE-MARK APPLIED FOR" but using the 1900-dated reverse. Probably the trademark came through sooner than he expected, for aside from a single example, this die was never used.

For further protection, Lesher filed for a design patent on February 14, which was granted on April 16. Though no size or value is specified, he had already decided to give in to complaints and change the face value to one dollar. As a result, the size was reduced and the weight cut to that of a standard silver dollar, 412½ grains. Another innovation was to leave a blank space to imprint a merchant's name in order to expand his business beyond

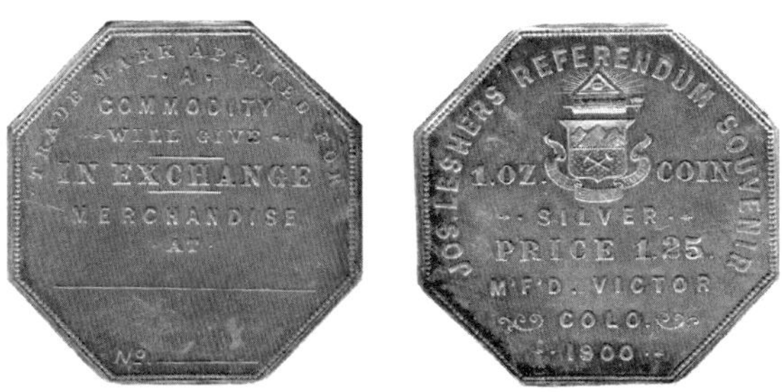

Pattern Lesher Dollar reading "TRADE-MARK APPLIED FOR." Actual size, 35 mm. *Courtesy of Christopher Marchase.*

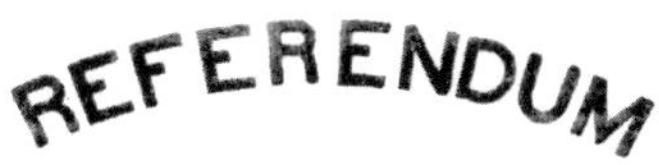

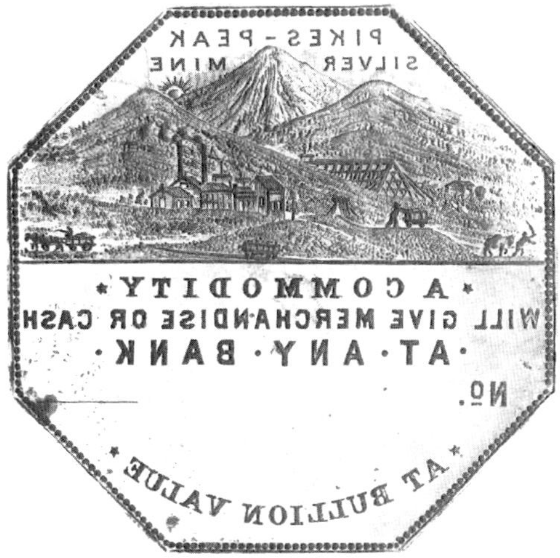

Above: REFERENDUM trademark "used since October 5, 1900," registered April 9, 1901. *Courtesy of U.S. Patent Office.*

Right: Reverse die for Bank type pattern, American Numismatic Society. *Courtesy of American Numismatic Society, New York.*

Below: *Courtesy of U.S. Patent Office.*

United States Patent Office.

JOSEPH LESHER, OF VICTOR, COLORADO.

TRADE-MARK FOR SILVER SOUVENIRS.

STATEMENT and DECLARATION of Trade-Mark No. 36,192, registered April 9, 1901.

Application filed February 14, 1901.

STATEMENT.

To all whom it may concern:

Be it known that I, Joseph Lesher, a citizen of the United States, residing at Victor, in the county of Teller and State of Colorado, and doing business at No. 511 West Victor avenue, in said city, have adopted for my use a Trade-Mark for Souvenirs, of which the following is a full, clear, and exact description.

My trade-mark consists of the arbitrary and fanciful word "Referendum." This has generally been arranged as shown in the accompanying facsimile-drawing, in which the word "Referendum" is printed in plain letters in a curved line. The style of lettering and arrangement of the word may be changed without altering the character of the trade-mark, the essential feature of which is the word "Referendum."

This trade-mark has been continuously used in my business since October 5, 1900.

The class to which this trade-mark is appropriated is souvenirs, and the particular description of goods comprised in such class upon which I use the said trade-mark is silver souvenirs.

The trade-mark is imprinted on the souvenirs and may be placed on boxes and packages containing the same.

JOSEPH LESHER.

Witnesses:
Sidney S. Garrison,
A. S. Lindholm.

DECLARATION.

State of Colorado, county of Teller, ss:

Joseph Lesher, being duly sworn, deposes and says that he is the applicant named in the foregoing statement; that he verily believes that the foregoing statement is true; that he has at this time a right to the use of the trade-mark therein described; that no other person, firm or corporation has the right to such use, either in the identical form or in any such near resemblance thereto as might be calculated to deceive; that it is used in commerce by him between the United States and foreign nations or Indian tribes, and particularly with Canada and that the description and the drawing presented for record truly represent the trade-mark sought to be registered.

JOSEPH LESHER.

Sworn to and subscribed before me this 25th day of January, 1901.

[L. S.] CLARENCE D. HALL,
Notary Public.

UNITED STATES PATENT OFFICE.

JOSEPH LESHER, OF VICTOR, COLORADO.

DESIGN FOR A SILVER SOUVENIR-MEDAL.

SPECIFICATION forming part of Design No. 34,359, dated April 16, 1901.

Application filed February 14, 1901. Serial No. 47,381. Term of patent 7 years.

To all whom it may concern:

Be it known that I, JOSEPH LESHER, a citizen of the United States, residing at Victor, in the county of Teller and State of Colorado, have invented and produced a new and original Design for a Silver Souvenir-Medal, of which the following is a specification.

My invention relates to a new and original design for a silver souvenir-medal, and is illustrated in the accompanying drawings, in which—

Figure 1 is a view of one side of the souvenir-medal, and Fig. 2 a view of the reverse or obverse side.

My design consists of a silver souvenir-medal having the features hereinafter described, reference being made to the accompanying drawings.

In said drawings the reference-numeral 1 designates the silver souvenir-medal, which is octagonal in shape, its eight sides 2 being straight and flat. On each face and along the eight edges thereof is an ornamental border 3.

One face of the souvenir is ornamented with a mountain scene 4 in cameo, consisting of three mountain peaks 5, with a sunburst 6 at the apex of one mountain, a trestle-work 7 nestled in the valley between the mountains, and a mill 8 in the foreground. The entrance 9 to a mine is shown at the base of one of the mountains, and mine-cars 10, a pack-mule 11, and a dray 12 appear in the foreground of the scene.

The reverse side of the souvenir is ornamented with a coat of arms 13.

My design presents a silver souvenir-medal of novel, pleasing, and attractive appearance.

Having thus described my invention, what I claim is—

The design for a souvenir-medal substantially as herein shown and described.

In testimony whereof I have hereunto set my hand in presence of two subscribing witnesses.

JOSEPH LESHER.

Witnesses:
SIDNEY S. GARRISON,
A. S. LINDHOLM.

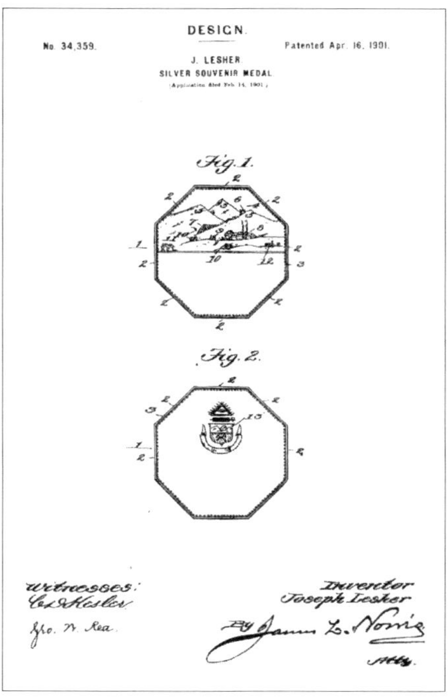

Above and left: Courtesy of U.S. Patent Office.

Below: Obverse die for Imprint Type. *Courtesy of American Numismatic Society, New York.*

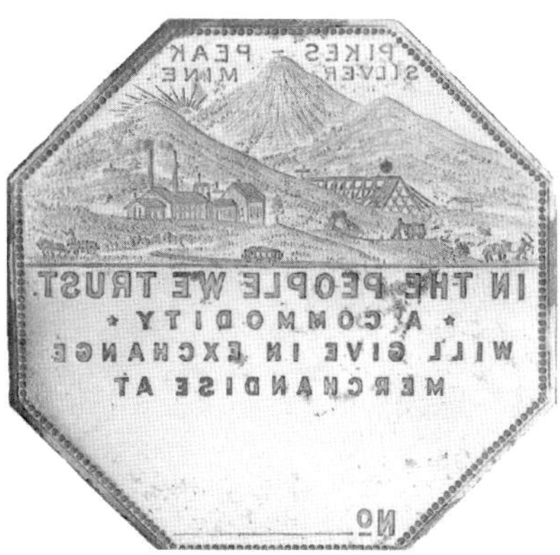

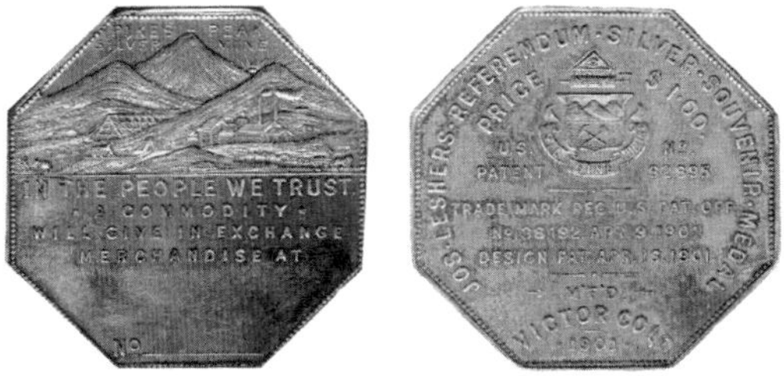

Actual size, 32 mm. *Courtesy of Christopher Marchase.*

Victor. (This decision was prescient, for A.B. Bumstead died suddenly on April 19, 1901, and his store was closed and liquidated.)

The reverse was redesigned to change the "price" to one dollar and the description to "silver souvenir medal." His trademark and design patent dates were mentioned, plus "U.S. Patent N°. 62,695." This is incorrect; this "patent" number is for a cooking stove invented in 1867 by Jacob H. Shear. It is a mystery as to how this error occurred. The obverse die and planchet cutter tools were discovered by Farran Zerbe "among discarded metal at a novelty works" and are now at the ANS.

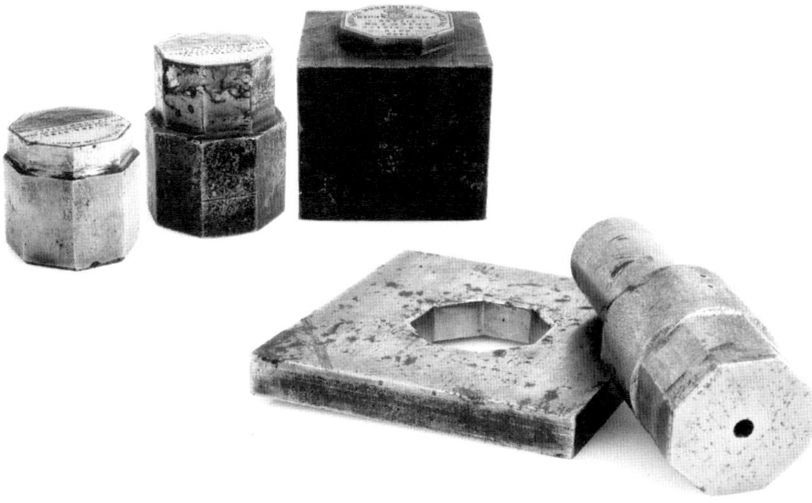

Planchet cutter and dies for various types of Lesher Dollars. *Courtesy of American Numismatic Society, New York.*

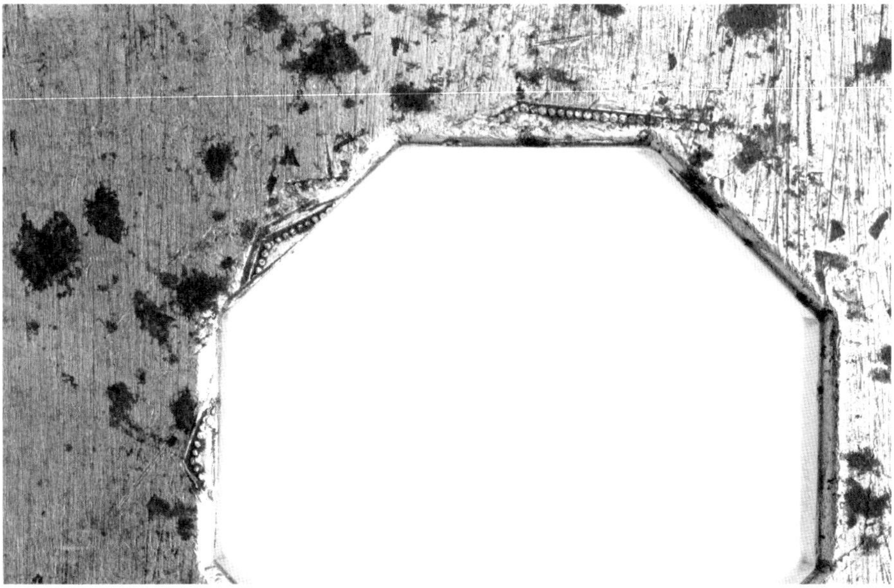

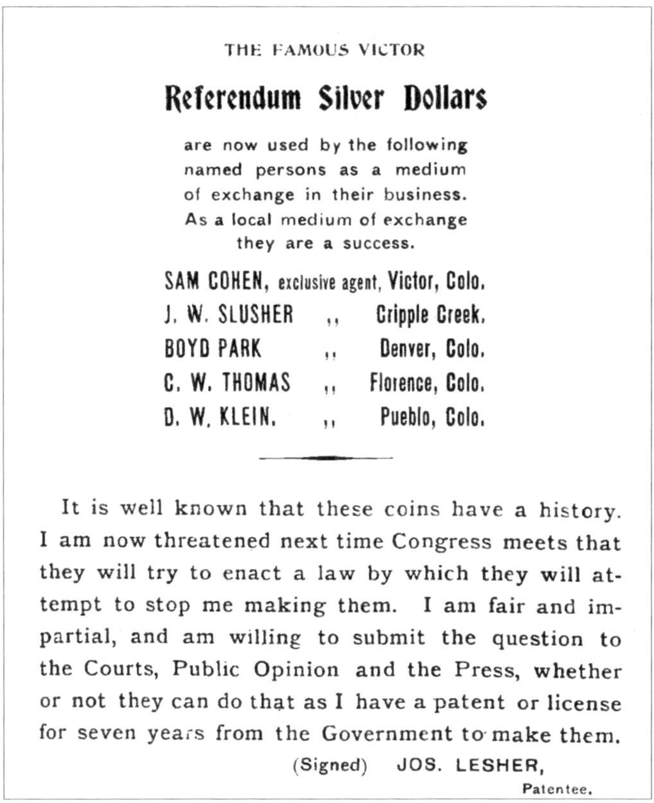

Above: Collar for Lesher Dollar, showing impressions of multiple misstrikes. *Courtesy of American Numismatic Society, New York.*

Left: Lesher's advertising card for Imprint-Type Lesher Dollars, 1901. *Courtesy of Dr. Philip W. Whiteley,* The Lesher Story.

Also found was the octagonal collar used to retain the planchets while being struck, called a "bed plate" by Zerbe. Lesher Dollars were coined by a weighted drop hammer, which fell from a height of several feet. After striking the blank, the operator had to catch the hammer on the bounce or it would strike a second time. This collar shows impressions of at least two misstrikes from missing the bounce.

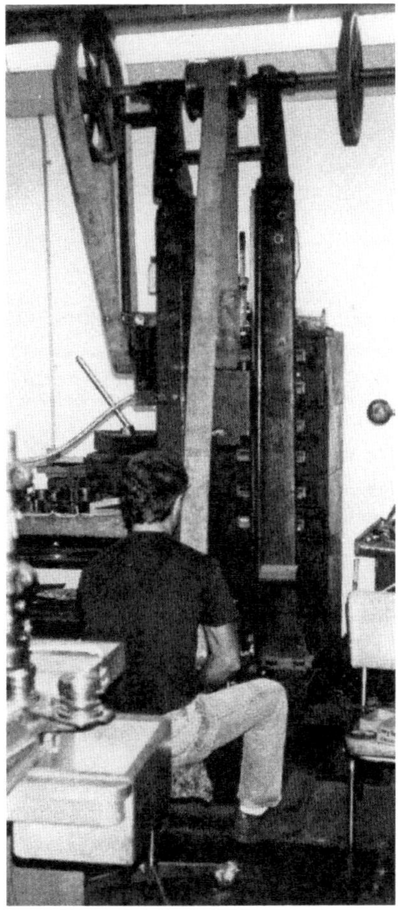

Drop hammer of same type used to strike Lesher Dollars in Denver. *American Numismatic Association, Colorado Springs.*

To distribute these Imprint-Type Dollars, Lesher appointed five "exclusive agents," printing a card to advertise them. Ten merchants signed on, and three other pieces are known with personalizations (see chapters 8–18). However, a regular system of numbering was not maintained, Lesher informed Zerbe; many pieces were unnumbered. While Lesher's orders are unreported, Adna Wilde estimated that about one thousand were issued.

The *Denver Post* of May 3, 1901, announced the release of the new issue for Boyd Park, Denver and J.M. Slusher, Cripple Creek. Lesher was still hoping "to establish channels for its circulation throughout the country," though in the end he had only a single customer outside Colorado.

Almost as an afterthought, the Denver office of the Secret Service closed out the Lesher Dollars file on June 9, 1901, without mentioning the latest issue. Special operative LaSalle quoted Bank of Victor receiving teller George T. Atkinson as stating "that the Joseph Lesher 'referendum dollar' excitement had almost entirely died out; that the coin had never been used in any other way only as a souvenir; that Bumstead the grocer took the coins in, the most of which were bought from him as souvenirs; that as much as three or four dollars had been paid for a single coin; that it was entirely untrue that

Lesher had deposited at their Bank a sum to cover the redemption of these coins; that none of these coins were redeemed by the Bank and that none were ever presented for redemption."

This is not quite true: avid collector Jean Maunovry (January 27, 1878–disappeared [!] September 21, 1921) wrote Zerbe that "the Referendums were accepted as a dollar in Cripple Creek, Victor, Colorado City and Colorado Springs, and even in Denver by some banks in a speculative way. I bought several from banks."

But Atkinson was right that interest was waning. Though the *Summit County (CO) Journal* carried an ad in the March 22, 1902 issue advising that jeweler M.G. Sacrider had "Lesher's Referendum silver souvenirs" and Lesher himself was mailing out his advertising card as late as 1903, the Imprint Type was never issued with a date later than 1901. The *Leadville Herald Democrat* responded to a correspondent on March 3, 1903, describing the Bumstead-type dollar and mentioning that one could be seen at the Carbonate Bank there. But it added, "For the benefit of our correspondent the Herald Democrat inquired of a Victor newspaper if these referendum coins were in use. Evidently Mr. Lesher and his 'referendum dollar' have passed into oblivion, for the newspaper people there knew nothing at all about the matter."

Though Lesher failed in his attempt to reopen closed silver mines, he foiled all efforts of the Secret Service to shut him down. No Lesher Dollars were ever seized; all that he lost was his first set of dies, and those were already obsolete—he was at the engraver's to have a new set made!

Chapter 5

Dies, Mintages and Survivors

Dies

The most diligent early Lesher Dollar researcher was well-known collector Farran Zerbe. He sought them actively, corresponded with other collectors and dealers and interviewed Lesher himself in 1914. In 1918, he published the most comprehensive catalogue of types in the *American Journal of Numismatics* 51 (1917).

Zerbe assigned catalogue numbers approximately in order of issue: First Type, 1900, 1; Bumstead (chapter 7), with scrolls, 2; Bumstead, no scrolls, 3; Bank Type, 4; Imprint Type, 1901 (blank), 5; Slusher (chapter 10), 6; Cohen (chapter 8), 7; Klein (chapter 14), 8; "Mullen" (chapter 9), 9; Boyd Park (chapter 12), 10; W.C. Alexander (chapter 15), 11; "Goodspeeds & Co." (chapter 16), 12. He did not assign separate numbers to numbered/unnumbered varieties or to those with no period after the number.

In the 1930s, two more stamped and engraved Imprint-Type dollars were discovered: J.E. Nelson (chapter 11) and W.F. White (chapter 17). Zerbe assigned these issues numbers 13 and 14, respectively, and while his updated catalogue was never published, his numbers became accepted.

In the catalogue of the 1952 American Numismatic Association (ANA) convention auction, John J. Ford Jr. gave a pseudo-Zerbe number to the engraved H. Stein piece (chapter 18) that he discovered in the O.K. Rumbel collection: 15. In 1958, Dr. Philip W. Whitely listed another engraved piece in his collection: H.H. Rosser (chapter 18) as "Zerbe No. 16." He also published the Trade-Mark Applied For Type for the first time but assigned it no pseudo-Zerbe number; however, Adna Wilde listed it as "Zerbe 17" in 1978.

The A.W. Clark engraved piece was rediscovered in 1998 (chapter 18) and has been designated "Zerbe 18."

Because of the imprinting or engraving of the issuers' names, however, all these types were struck from a very limited number of dies, five obverses and four reverses:

Lesher Dollar Dies

Zerbe No.	Obverse Die	Reverse Die
1	Z1O	Z1R
2	Z2O	Z2R
3	Z2O	Z3R
4	Z4O	Z3R
17	Z17O	Z3R
5	Z5O	Z5R
6	Z5O	Z5R
7	Z5O	Z5R
8	Z5O	Z5R
9	Z5O	Z5R
10	Z5O	Z5R
11	Z5O	Z5R
12	Z5O	Z5R
13	Z5O	Z5R
14	Z5O	Z5R
15	Z5O	Z5R
16	Z5O	Z5R
18	Z5O	Z5R

The disposition of these 9 dies, as nearly as can be determined, is:

Disposition of Lesher Dollar Dies

Die No.	Disposition
Z1O	Seized by Secret Service, November 19, 1900
Z1R	Seized by Secret Service, November 19, 1900
Z2O	Presumed discarded by Mrs. Lesher, 1933
Z2R	Broke — replaced by Z3R
Z3R	ANS 41.173 — Zerbe gift
Z4O	ANS 41.173 — Zerbe gift
Z17O	Presumed discarded by Mrs. Lesher, 1933
Z5O	ANS 41.173 — Zerbe gift
Z5R	Presumed discarded by Mrs. Lesher, 1933

As mentioned in the previous chapter, the dies for the first type of Lesher Dollar were seized by the Secret Service on November 19, 1900. Though no record has been located, they were presumably sent to Washington and destroyed. Die Z2R broke in the course of production and was replaced by Z3R, which still survives, together with Z4O and Z5O. These three dies were purchased by Zerbe from Joseph Lesher in 1914 and donated to the American Numismatic Society in 1941.

In an inventory dated July 23, 1918, Zerbe wrote that he had acquired "Lesher's—3 dies—2 punches and 3 bed plates. (1 die Obv. The rare 'At any Bank.' Only 5 struck [however, 10 are known]. Rev. owned by Lesher—rusted." (The reverse die retained by Lesher was not the reverse of the Bank Type, however, which was Z3R, but the reverse of the Imprint Type, Z5R.)

As for the remaining dies, Farran Zerbe wrote to Mrs. Lesher on October 31, 1934: "At the time I called on Mr. Lesher I obtained from his [*sic*] some of the dies (blocks of iron with devise engraved on them) that were used in striking the pieces. There were other dies that he retained. Do you have them or know what became of them?" She replied on November 6:

> *Am sorry to inform you that I do not know where any of the dies are. I had my Wood shed turned into a living room last spring and remembering seeing*

some or part of the dies and cannot remember what I did with them and cannot get around to hunt them up [she had broken her hip and was on crutches]. *I am quite sure that Mr. Lesher left the face, or* [octagon drawn]. *But cannot remember when I saw It last and think I threw the others over the Dump. We had them so long around the house That I had tired of moving them* [around] *and being so helpless I cannot think when I saw them last. Am awful sorry.*

MINTAGES

The number of Lesher Dollars minted—both original and net—is not known. According to Lesher Dollar enthusiast Charles E. Briggs, who visited Lesher in 1913, "He had kept no records as to the number of pieces struck or number of dies used." However, Lesher estimated that "between 2000 and 3000 were struck."

Farran Zerbe visited him the following year and was now told that "about 3500, including all types, were struck," but "[w]hen [Lesher] was interviewed personally…in many instances his memory serves only for approximate answers to direct questions." Zerbe estimated that, "allowing for some believed to have been melted, the distribution was probably about 3000 pieces."

This would seem to be fairly definitive, but Adna G. Wilde, Jr. concluded, after making an exhaustive study, that only 1,869 Lesher Dollars—of all types—were issued. He postulated that 1,050 Imprint-Type Lesher Dollars were made, including those stamped or engraved, later revising this to "about 1000."

For the Bumstead Type, Wilde thought that there were only 210 made with scrolls and 500 without scrolls, for a total of 710, based on the serial numbers recorded. However, there are large gaps in the serial numbering: the 300s and 400s are missing, as are the 1100s, 1200s, 1300s, 1400s and 1600s. The *Victor Daily Record* for December 9, 1900, reported that Lesher returned from Denver on December 8 with "1,000 pieces, and within five hours he had disposed of 800 of them in the district." An illustration of Bumstead dollar No. 510 accompanied the story. Another order, unreported, probably followed.

In a few months, however, A.B. Bumstead was dead and his store closed. Lesher had apparently already decided to switch to the $1.00 face-value Imprint Type. If he returned 800 $1.25 pieces for melting, he would have had enough silver to mint all 1,000 Imprint Types, with some left over for loss in melting. Perhaps fewer than that were returned for recoinage, but if 700 or 800 struck pieces were melted, Wilde's total rises to about 2,570 or 2,670—about in line with Lesher's 1913 estimate and not far from Zerbe's of the following year. Thus, Wilde's figure would refer to the net mintage, not the total struck.

SURVIVORS

In 1978, Wilde knew of just 384 pieces, but as of the date of this writing, the total is about 600. This is less than a third of the total issued. Where are the rest?

Chapter 6

A "Lesher Dollar Treasure"?

All these missing coins led to a story of a Lesher Dollar treasure. The November 21, 2008 issue of the *Colorado Springs News* carried an article by Bill Vogrin: "Mystery of the Lesher Dollars." It gives the account of treasure hunter W.C. Jameson, who wrote about the stash in his book *Colorado Treasure Tales* (Caxton Press, 2001). In his book, "Jameson says Lesher's silver coins were hoarded by Victor businessman Zach Hutton," Vogrin wrote. Jameson believed that "hundreds" were waiting to be found.

Per Vogrin's summary, "'Hutton did not quite understand the purpose and the intended temporary nature of the coins,' Jameson wrote in his book. 'Hutton believed the Lesher dollars were actually produced by the United States government and he perceived them as real money.'" So he saved then in two large coffee cans. "'By the end of 1901, Hutton completely filled the cans with the dollars,' Jameson wrote. 'Concerned someone might want to steal his collection of Lesher dollars, estimated to be several hundred by now, Hutton hid them someplace on his property.' In January 1902, Hutton died of pneumonia."

According to Vogrin, "Jameson and his looters ransacked Hutton's business and home in Victor in search of the stash. They pulled up floorboards and ripped open the walls hunting for the coins. They were never found."

Unfortunately, Vogrin misunderstood a key aspect of Jameson's account: in this carelessly edited book (the Contents reads "Lost Confederate [*sic*!] Coins Worth $$," while the chapter title has "Lost Counterfeit Coins Now Worth $$$), Jameson made it clear that the break-in at Hutton's house occurred "not long after his [Hutton's] funeral" in 1902, not by "Jameson and his looters" in recent years.

(There are other errors in *Colorado Treasure Tales*, not worth mentioning here. Jameson gave no authority for the Lesher treasure story in his book, but in an interview with Vogrin for the article, "Jameson said he came upon journal notes and a diary that described Hutton and his stash of Lesher dollars. 'I lived in Woodland Park about six years, and I spent time around Victor working on that story,' he said. 'I chased down some things, looking for historical connections, interviewing people. I was in possession of that story a good long time before I wrote it.'")

However that may be, Jameson's primary source would appear to be "Lost Cache of Rare Lesher Dollars" by Ken Weinman in *Lost Treasure* (December 1993). For example, Weinman wrote, "Zachary Hutton, a local businessman, did not understand completely the purpose of the Lesher dollars....He stashed them away as though they were coins issued by the U.S. Mint." Jameson wrote, "Businessman Zach Hutton, did not quite understand the purpose and the intended temporary nature of the coins. Hutton believed the Lesher dollars were actually produced by the United States government."

So we will focus on Weinman's account and not Jameson's rewrite. In this version, Zachary Hutton, a miser who "consistently saved most of his money," knew Joseph Lesher.

> *Several times Lesher tried to convince Hutton to spend the coins, returning them to active circulation, their purpose in the first place. Hutton would not spend them, and took all the Lesher dollars he could get his hands on and stored them in two large empty salt pork tins* [sic].
>
> *During the cold, wet winter of 1902, Hutton took sick and died of pneumonia. He was a bachelor and had no living relatives that anyone knew of. Though several people searched his property, the two tin cans full of Lesher Dollars were never found.*

(Note that Weinman does not give January 1902 specifically as when Hutton became ill nor that the search of his property was the result of a break-in, implying that it was done by agents of the court. However, it is possible Jameson had an additional source, as he claimed.)

Weinman's primary source was given as "Ferguson. *Treasure World.* 1973." This is a misprint for Jeff Ferguson's article "Colorado's Cache of Rare Lesher Dollars" in *Treasure World* (December–January 1975), page 26.

Ferguson, the author of two brief articles in this issue, gave no authority for his account either. (He was a very prolific writer of articles for treasure hunting magazines in the 1970s, and one researcher denounced all of his shipwreck stories as "pure fiction." But perhaps he was better informed as to Colorado treasures.) Weinman's version followed it closely, except that Ferguson identified Zachary Hutton as a Victor cobbler and did not describe the salt pork tins as "large."

Ferguson's cache story is plausible, and just possibly there is another reference to it somewhere. However, it is not without serious problems: Zachary Hutton didn't exist! The U.S. census of Colorado for 1900 lists no "Zachary Hutton" anywhere in the state, nor is there a death record for any Zachary Hutton in Teller County (Victor) for 1901–3. No one of this name had a store in downtown Victor in 1900. Lesher Dollar researcher Chris Marchase did research in the Dun business directories and never found his name listed in Cripple Creek, Victor or any other towns in the district. Nor are there any deaths by pneumonia during this period, of any name, that match Ferguson's account. Is the whole story fiction?

As mentioned in the previous chapter, though it would appear that close to two thousand Lesher Dollars were issued, only about six hundred are known. Are "hundreds" of them really buried somewhere in Colorado "in two empty salt pork tins"?

Salt pork was not canned but shipped dry in kegs or sacks, so Jameson's understanding of "empty salt pork tins" as "coffee cans" is incorrect; these would have been more or less rectangular large containers, capable of holding up to twenty-five pounds of salt pork each. Calculating the exact number of Lesher Dollars that could fit in this space is problematic because by 1901 they had been coined in two sizes. However, the total mintage could probably fit in such containers. So the possibility that hundreds of Lesher Dollars have been buried since 1902 cannot be dismissed.

Coauthor Ken Hallenbeck recalls:

> *This story brings to mind a situation which occurred when I first came to Colorado Springs in 1978 or so. I was interested in Leshers at that time and a guy had come in to ANA Headquarters there claiming to have a coffee can full of Lesher Dollars. He came in several times (but always when I was out) to show me some of them. But whenever I actually saw him, he never had any with him. So I finally concluded that he was just jerking my chain. But the possibility of the tin can full of Leshers might actually have been a reality. We'll never know. After all these years I have no idea of who*

> *the guy was. But he was a pleasant person is all that I can remember. But with this said, it adds a slight bit of credence to the story of the coffee cans full of Leshers.*

There are two other stories of Lesher Dollar hoards. Jean Maunovry, formerly of Denver but later of Rochester, New York, "purchased from one person a lot of about one hundred in 1905, and several at different times from banks, curio shops, and individuals." As of November 9, 1934, Farran Zerbe made no mention of this hoard in his revised article, perhaps believing it to have been dispersed, since Maunovry was a coin dealer.

In Dr. Philip W. Whiteley's 1958 booklet, *The Lesher Story*, he remarked, "We also know that there are seventeen (17) Klein pieces and six (6) Alexanders in one heretofore [un?]exposed hoard. This may change the complexion of the rarity if these pieces are made available." They have never appeared, but a clue as to ownership will be found in chapter 15. Perhaps this hoard is the unseen "coffee can treasure."

Chapter 7

A.B. Bumstead, Popular Grocer of Victor

Arthur Bolles Bumstead was an obscure Victor grocer until he immortalized himself by visiting Referendum Souvenir issuer Joseph Lesher on the morning of November 13, 1900 (chapter 4). "[Bumstead] proposed to accept the souvenirs in exchange for groceries and give them out to anyone who wanted them in change." Lesher at once accepted and turned his entire remaining inventory over to him; he was so relieved that he planned to have a new die made, naming Bumstead as their redeemer.

With some changes in wording, and a new design, such dies were ordered and a reported 1,000 pieces released in Victor on December 8, 1900. (As mentioned in chapter 5, the number actually minted is uncertain. Recorded numbers range from 20 [only one this low], 101 to 604 for the first type, with scrolls [no 300s or 400s] and 600 to 1026 for the second type, without scrolls, plus 1535, 1536, 1740 and 1741. From these numbers, Adna Wilde thought that the total struck was 210 with scrolls and 500 without, but this is surely too low. Based on Lesher's recollections, there was probably a further order, with as many as 700 or 800 melted to obtain silver to mint the Imprint Type.) As illustrated in chapter 4, these Lesher Dollars read "WILL GIVE IN EXCHANGE MERCHANDISE AT A.B. BUMSTEAD."

While Arthur was growing up, his father apparently lost three successive farms in three states; this may have influenced his later sentiment for inflation and Free Silver. Arthur was born on a farm in Maremont, Indiana, on December 19, 1863, to John A. Bumstead and Maryetta "Etta" (Alden) Foote Bumstead. In 1870, the Bumsteads were living in Union Township, Marshall County, Indiana, with two children and real estate worth $600, no personal estate. But the post–Civil War depression seemingly did them in, for within five years, they had moved to Kansas.

On March 1, 1875, the Kansas state census listed the Bumstead family at Quito, Little River Township, in Butler County. (By 1916, the entire town of Quito was extinct, its former site located on Peter Johnson's farm on Little Walnut.) No value was shown for real estate, and John's personal estate was a paltry eighty-eight dollars. Chapters of the Grange—a farmers' movement to raise the social and economic position of farmers and negotiate better railroad freight rates and grain storage charges—were being organized in Butler County that year, and Mrs. Bumstead was appointed secretary of the Valley View Grange in Quito.

But the Grange was powerless to save the Quito farms from drought, chinch bugs and grasshoppers, and later that year or in 1876, John Bumstead moved his family to Nebraska. Presumably he farmed there too, though no record has been located. The census of 1880 found him in Lincoln, Nebraska, now working as a laborer. Arthur was able to obtain some schooling through all these moves (only three months in 1874–75, though), but his father struggled to support the family, trying one occupation after another.

At the age of twenty, Arthur was a bookkeeper for the same employer his father worked for as a shipping clerk, butter and egg man J.L. Osborne; he was still living at home in Lincoln. By 1886, he had taken a job as bookkeeper for the Lincoln firm of Plummer, Perry & Co., wholesale grocers. He remained with them, learning the grocery business, until 1891.

On August 21, 1886, Arthur married Ida May Poste of Lincoln. They started a family and had an active social life there. On January 31, 1889, Seely H. Hoag—a grocer in Colorado Springs—married Arthur's cousin Harriet "Hattie" Carrie Bumstead. She was the daughter of John A. Bumstead's brother, Edwin Stimson Bumstead. Arthur and S.H. probably met at the wedding and became friends because of their common interest in the grocery business.

When the Cripple Creek gold rush began in 1891, Arthur moved to Colorado Springs to form a retail grocery partnership with his cousin. S.H. Hoag seems always to have been the senior partner; the *1892 Colorado Springs City Directory* lists the grocery as Hoag & Bumstead. A meat market had been added by the time the 1894 directory was surveyed.

The bigger opportunity was in the Cripple Creek District itself, however, so in 1895, "the firm removed to Victor to engage in the same business," according to Bumstead's obituary. Probably Hoag owned the store building, which he rented to Bumstead, who conducted the grocery in his own name.

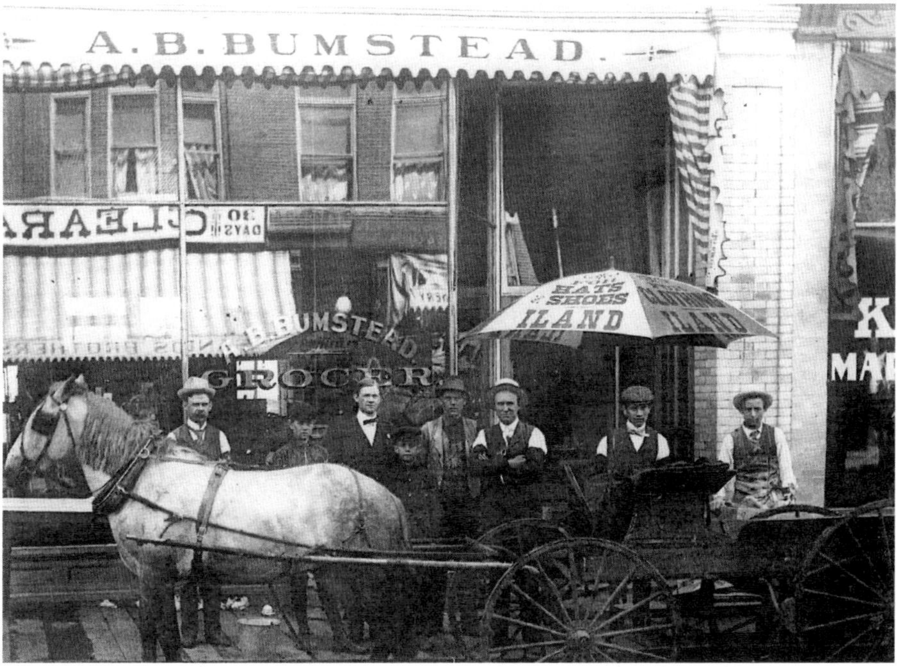

A.B. Bumstead's grocery, 110 North Third Street, Victor, Colorado, circa 1900. *Left to right*: clerk, son Carl Bumstead (twelve), A.B. Bumstead [below E in GROCER], son John Alden Bumstead (ten) and four clerks. *Courtesy of John Alden Bumstead.*

In any case, the *1896 Colorado Springs City Directory* has the curious entry "Bumstead A.B., grocer at Victor, res 420 East Cache la Poudre st. [Colorado Springs]." S.H. Hoag was not listed and may have been in Victor. Bumstead is shown at this address in the *1898 Colorado Springs City Directory* also, and his son Lucius Allen was born there on November 22, 1898. Apparently he kept his family in Colorado Springs while he ran the grocery in Victor, which was no place for children then.

The *1896 Victor City Directory* lists his grocery as A.B. Bumstead and Co., grocers, with Bumstead's residence the same as his store. He was still using this style on August 21, 1899, when his stock was "wiped out" by the fire of 1899; his business had reached "large proportions" by then, per his obituary in the *Daily Record*. "Undaunted by the loss, Mr. Bumstead re-engaged in the same business alone and had met with the success which his great energy, his indomitable will and his straightforward, honorable methods could not but bring," the *Daily Record* gushed.

The reference to "alone" in the obituary is explained by Bumstead's ad in the *Victor Evening Times* on September 9, 1899. He announced "a successor to the firm of A.B. Bumstead & Co.…A.B. Bumstead With Victor Produce Company." He also stated that due to the "great expense" of handling a credit business he had "decided to do a strictly Spot Cash Business." (This was easier said than done, for when his business was wound up less than two years later, there were at least 185 unsettled credit accounts on the books.) Within a year, he had relocated again, to 110 North Third Street.

About 1900, he issued his first numismatic item, an aluminum token reading A.B. BUMSTEAD/ GROCER/ VICTOR, COLO. on the obverse and GOOD FOR ONE TEN CENT LOAF BREAD on the other. Such tokens were common for merchants in remote areas with spotty access to coins, though this particular one may have been issued as part of a promotion of some kind. (One of these tokens was "washed up by the rain" in July 2007, roughly a block from where Bumstead's store stood.)

The second and third types of Lesher Dollars, December 8, 1900, are in effect tokens also, nominally good for "merchandise" there—but their huge silver content served to give them general circulation.

Unlike many other Lesher Dollar issuers, Bumstead was a true blueblood, through his mother tenth in descent from *Mayflower* passengers John Alden and Priscilla Mullins. He was well aware of his heritage, naming his second son John Alden Bumstead after his ancestor.

Sadly, on April 11, 1901, Bumstead fell ill with pneumonia. He expired at 8:20 a.m. on April 19, and his body was sent to Wyuka Cemetery, Lincoln, Nebraska, for burial. Both the *Victor Daily Record* and the *Victor Daily Times* published extensive obituaries.

The *Daily Record* characterized him as "one of [Victor's] most substantial and progressive business men. Mr. Bumstead was an active worker in every line that was of benefit to the city. His friends were measured by the hundreds. He was not only popular with his own people but the travelling public and especially the commercial men, thought a great deal of him, and made his store their headquarters while in the city. Mr. Bumstead was active, courteous and obliging." The *Daily Times* added that "no man in the community [had] more friends or firmer friends than he."

Hoag, who was also sick—he moved from Colorado Springs to Fort Collins for his health in 1900—lost no time in selling out Bumstead's business. (Hoag himself succumbed on December 8, 1901, less than eight months after his partner.) Everything was liquidated, including stock and fixtures. When the estate was settled in June 1902, Mrs. Bumstead had received her widow's allowance of $1,685, but the balance of $8,844.91 was apparently paid to Seely H. Hoag's heirs.

Chapter 8

Sam Cohen, Jeweler and Agent for Victor

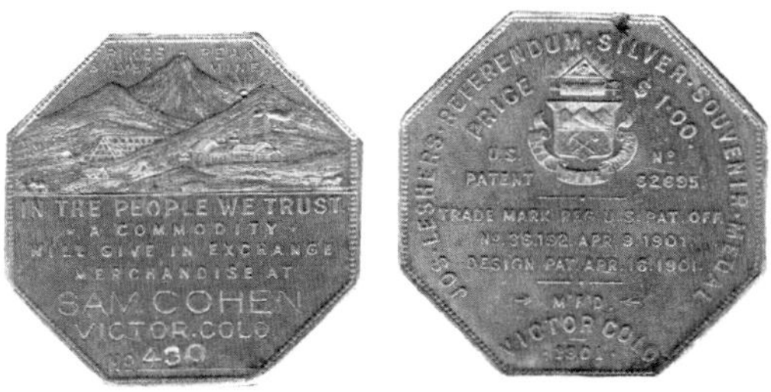

As mentioned in chapter 4, Joseph Lesher did not want the bother of selling his Referendum Silver Dollars individually, so he appointed five "exclusive agents" to distribute them. Of these, the first was Sam Lewis ("Sam") Cohen of Victor, Colorado, whose Lesher Dollars are marked SAM COHEN/ VICTOR, COLO. This is his story.

Life was hard for Jews under the czars. Following the partitions of Poland in 1772, 1793 and 1795, 900,000 Jews became subjects of Russia. But they were not permitted to live beyond the Pale of Settlement, to the west and south of Holy Mother Russia itself. After 1805, the Pale began to be reduced, and Jews who had been permitted to settle in Russian cities were forced back into small villages and banned from their professions. In 1827, Jewish boys became subject to lifetime military conscription.

As a result, energetic Russian Jews began to abandon anti-Semitic Russia and immigrate to the United States. Among these pioneers was Jacob Cohen (circa 1842–May 17, 1896), who disembarked at New York from the *Calabria* with his family on March 27, 1871. He pushed westward to Minneapolis, then a booming sawmilling and flour milling center of fifteen thousand, becoming the first Russian Jew to settle there.

Actual size, 32 mm. *Courtesy of Christopher Marchase.*

Not long afterward, Louis Cohen (*Elazar ben Shimon Meir*, circa 1848–September 29, 1894), another Russian Jew and perhaps a younger brother of Jacob, settled in Minneapolis also. There he apparently met his wife, Ida Volaska (surname unknown), born in Germany about seven years after him. He opened a confectionery in downtown Minneapolis, at the corner of Main Street and Second Avenue Southeast, East Division. His son Mier Haskell was born on September 16, 1875, and Sam Lewis followed on October 4, 1877.

But Louis apparently began to show symptoms of consumption (tuberculosis), the leading cause of death in the United States at that time, and his confectionery was last listed in the Minneapolis city directory for 1876; probably he lost customers afraid of contagion. For the next five years or so, he seemingly roamed around, seeking a cure. Louis finally settled on Denver, reputed to be the best place for consumptives. (By 1900, according to historian Cynthia Stout, "one-third of Colorado's population were residents of the state because of tuberculosis.") He switched to the grocery business but was either weak or felt the need to avoid customers because of coughing blood, so his wife began to run it in her name, though Louis was sometimes shown as "manager." Still, he recovered enough from the dry air that they had another child, Sarah (Sadye), in July 1884.

Around 1889, the family moved to Pueblo, a slightly lower elevation than Denver. Mrs. Cohen may have gone first to pick a location for the grocery and get started while Louis remained in Denver for a time; they lived apart at times in the early 1890s. On September 29, 1894, Louis died at home at the early age of forty-six.

The younger son of this pioneer was Sam Cohen. In early 1896, his older brother was studying medicine at the University of Minnesota while he was just a teenage clerk in his widowed mother's Pueblo grocery store. But ten years later, it was Sam who was so wealthy that he was essentially able to retire.

On April 27, 1896, Sam—still a teenager, though nearly six feet tall—left the Florence and Cripple Creek Railroad station in Cripple Creek, with his .38 Smith & Wesson revolver and his dog, Pondo, to seek his fortune, delighted by the wonderful scenery he saw en route but appalled by his fellow passengers: drunken, profane men and "hard looking women," he later wrote.

In a short time, he moved to nearby Victor and immediately opened a grocery store, the only business he knew, where he also roomed. But Sam quickly saw that luxury goods had better prospects in this gold mining boomtown. Miners were well paid: wages averaged about $4 per day, and they were supplemented by "high-grading"—stealing ore from the mines. An adept high-grader could increase his income by as much as $100 a day. And the mine owners, of course, did far better: Winfield Scott Stratton, owner of the fabulous Independence Mine, decided to *limit* his profits to $2,000 per day in order to extend the life of the mine.

So young Sam set out to learn the jewelry business, probably by working as a clerk in one of the local stores. He founded Sam Cohen & Co., Jewelers, by late 1898, advertising "Xmas Specials" in the *Victor Evening Times* on December 13, 1898. Sam became so successful that his mother and sister moved from Pueblo to join him. His brother Mier Haskell followed in 1899 after graduating from Bellevue Hospital College in New York and began practicing medicine in Victor.

By 1900, they could afford an Irish servant girl. But later that year, disaster struck: the entire business district burned down. On the afternoon of August 21, a woman in a brothel in Victor's notorious Paradise Alley on Third Avenue was, as Sam Cohen himself put it, "cleaning her dress with naphtha while blithely smoking a cigarette. An unsteady hand, shaking from too much absinthe the night before, spilled the can of naphtha and the lighted cigarette did the rest." The fire burned for hours in a great circle, destroying a dozen or more square blocks. The flames were fanned by a "gale," and—as construction then was virtually all of pine—everything burned quickly and completely. The fire department was helpless; even dynamiting failed because the wind-swept embers set new fires.

The *Cripple Creek Morning Times* reported on August 22 that Sam Cohen's loss was $5,000, with insurance of $2,500. And his store wasn't the only casualty. "As I started for home late that afternoon," he wrote, "I noticed some sheets of music blowing around on the street. On picking them up I recognized them as coming from my home which had burned to the ground."

But the citizens of Victor were not easily defeated. Like those of Cripple Creek, who had suffered not one but two devastating fires three years before, they began to recover at once. The former site of Sam Cohen's jewelry store and the Palace Market was to be rebuilt with a large brick block, it was announced on August 24. Sam didn't wait; the *Morning Times* of August 25 reported that he had "put most of his jewelry in a big safe, and it passed through the fire without a nickel's damage. He will resume business in a tent to-day."

When the brick block was finished, he moved in. A photograph dated "August 1900," but clearly later, shows his new store at 305 Victor Avenue,

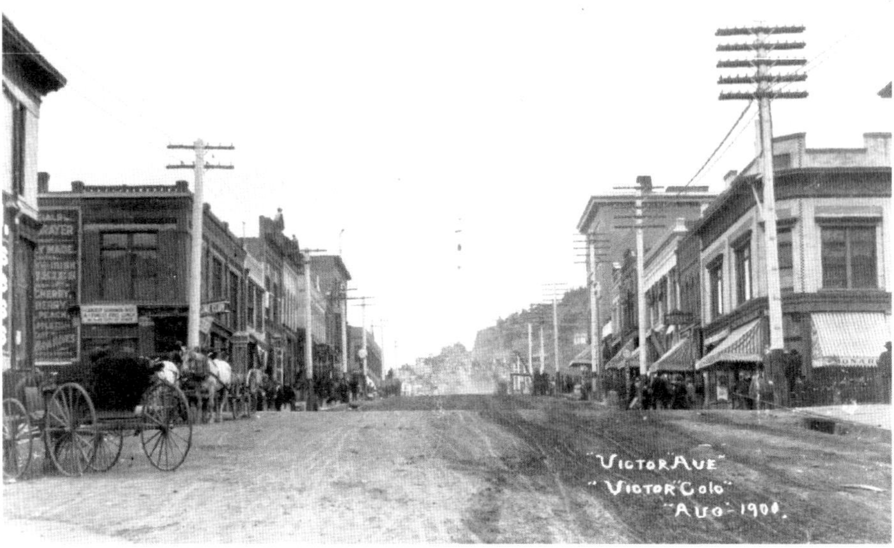

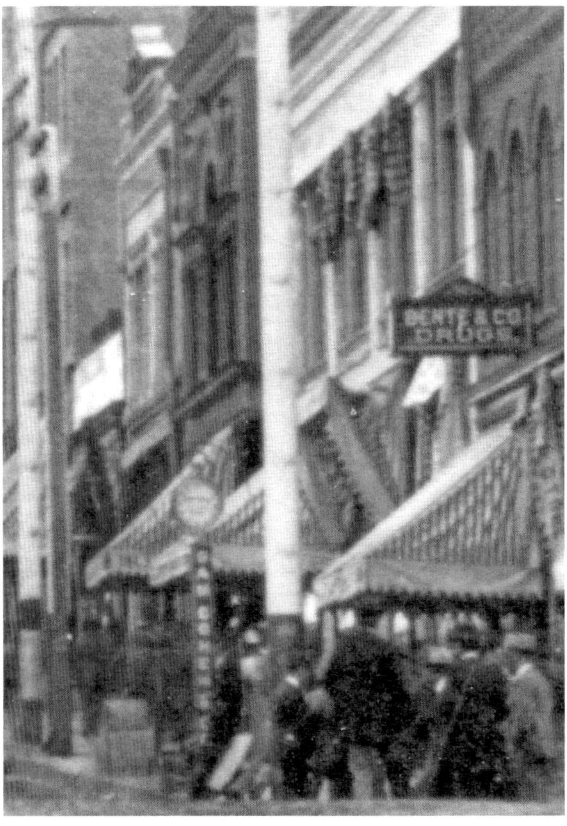

Above: Victor Avenue, Victor, August 1900, showing the new store of Sam Cohen & Co. at 305 Victor Avenue, just west of Bente & Co. Drugs. Cohen's sign is a pole outside his store reading SAM COHEN & CO. vertically, surmounted by a giant watch. *Courtesy of Cripple Creek District Museum.*

Left: *Courtesy of Cripple Creek District Museum.*

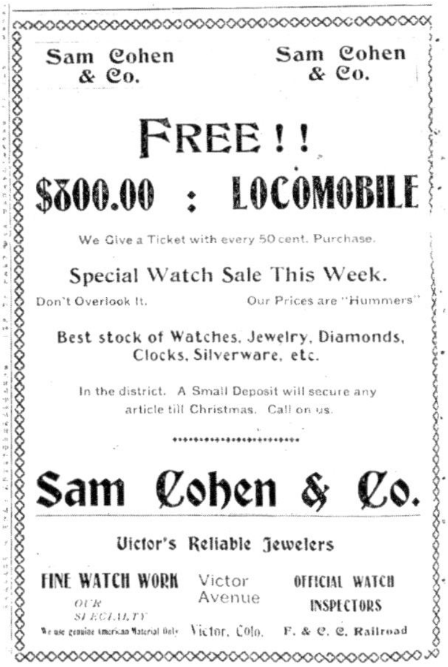

Cohen ad in the *Victor Daily Herald*, November 21, 1900, offering chances to win a free car. Victor Daily Herald, *November 21, 1900.*

just west of Bente & Co., Drugs. His sign was a pole in front reading SAM COHEN & CO. vertically, surmounted by a giant watch. In November 1900, he advertised for a "first class watchmaker and engraver," and Nathan M. Cohen Jr. of Pueblo, another second-generation Russian Jew and perhaps a relative or school friend, worked for him as a clerk from 1901 to 1904.

Not content with the usual advertising claims of superiority, Sam Cohen offered chances to win a free car in his ad in the *Victor Daily Herald* on November 21, 1900. Another venture was acting as an "exclusive agent" for Victor for Joseph Lesher's "Referendum Silver Dollars" from 1901 to 1903. The Cripple Creek District was "red hot" for the free coinage of silver at the ratio of sixteen to one, in spite of its dependence on gold, Cohen wrote. He admired Lesher for refusing to admit the defeat of free coinage following the reelection of William McKinley in 1900 and making silver "dollars" himself.

So Cohen signed on as an agent for the one-dollar series dated 1901, agreeing to redeem any presented for merchandise. But after a short time, he reported, ardor cooled: "Soon, however, these Lesher souvenir 'dollars' disappeared from circulation and got into the hands of numismatists."

By July 1906, R.G. Dun & Co.'s *Reference Book* listed S. Cohen & Co., Jewelers, with a credit rating of D 1½ (pecuniary strength $35,000 to $50,000, general credit high). In addition, Sam had, with partners, taken a lease on the Independence Mine "after it ceased to be operated on company account." His brother Haskell was chief surgeon to the Independence Mine and physician to the Portland Gold Mining Company from about 1902 to December 1, 1905.

Sam Cohen was sympathetic to the gold miner's union and mentions sitting alongside the feared "Big Bill" Haywood, secretary of the Western Federation of Miners and later co-founder of the Industrial Workers of the World (IWW), "many times" at the lunch counter of a restaurant in

Victor. He "watched spellbound union waiters serve their master with an awe comparable only to that inspired by a Stalin, a Hitler, or a Mussolini."

This union was known for its violent methods. In 1902, "several men who opposed the Federation were found murdered, their bodies at the bottom of abandoned mine shafts." Governor Stuenenberg of Idaho was assassinated by a dynamite bomb at his home December 30, 1905, as a result of his imposing martial law (in April 1899) to halt a strike by the Western Federation of Miners; the bomber said that the killing was ordered by Haywood and two others. And on June 6, 1904, Cohen himself witnessed the aftermath of the dynamiting of non-union miners waiting for a train to take them home; thirteen or more men were killed instantly, many blown to bits, and others were horribly maimed. No one was ever convicted of this outrage, but it led to such revulsion that the union's power was destroyed.

By 1906, Cohen could see that returns from the mines were diminishing. He left Victor a wealthy man, only returning the next year to visit the Portland Mine, in which he apparently had an interest. About this time, he moved to New York, his mother and sister following; his brother moved his medical practice to Denver. In 1908, Sam enrolled in the New York Law School, New York City, earning his LLB in 1910 and, in June 1911, his LLM. The following year, he was admitted to the New York bar.

Without connections, Cohen had to take a job as "Legal Adjuster" for a traveling circus (Billie Nelson Show), per *Billboard* of March 23, 1912, upon being admitted to the bar. But by the next year, he had set up a private practice of law at 115 Broadway, New York, though he was still living with his mother and his sister's family. In 1919, he joined the new law firm of Moses & Singer, New York, still in business, and remained there until 1956, when he applied for Social Security.

Around 1916, he married Rose Hirschfeld of Buffalo, New York, who was about thirty years old. She presented him with two sons: Lewis H. Cohen, 1919, and John M. Cohen, 1922.

Cohen prospered at Moses & Singer: by 1935, the family was living at 1136 Fifth Avenue in Manhattan with a live-in butler and cook. The next year, Sam took the whole family on a cruise to Bermuda, perhaps in celebration of his twentieth wedding anniversary.

Rose predeceased him on February 28, 1951, in New York, and he also died there in December 1965, at age eighty-eight.

In 1940, Sam L. Cohen self-published *Gold Rush De Luxe*, a book of reminiscences of his decade in the Cripple Creek Mining District. Most concern his arrival in Cripple Creek and adventures in Victor, but four pages are devoted to the Lesher Dollar.

In the final section, on "The Future of Gold," he was eerily prescient about economic matters. He wrote:

> *The...Government* [is] *able to enforce low interest rates which permit* [it] *to outbid private banks in increasing categories of financing and which penalize those who do not deserve punishment—millions of thrifty persons who deposit their earnings in savings banks and the holders of life insurance policies, the former by interest rates on their savings being reduced to the vanishing point. * * Many savings banks have reduced interest to 1½% per annum, while Government bonds and notes issued by the Government have been sold at an interest rate as low as ¾%.*

Cohen blamed this situation on the government's seizing all the gold in the United States and reburying it in Fort Knox, which took money matters out of the hands of the people and transferred control to government printing presses.

Despite his many successes in business and the bar, Cohen was a disappointment to Lesher as an agent; in 1914, Lesher told Farran Zerbe that Cohen bought but "a few small lots at different times." Among these would be the fifty he used himself (numbers in the range of 403–441 reported); probably the fifty or one hundred (numbers in the range of 1502–1550, plus three unnumbered) sold to Geo. McMullen, a Victor shoemaker (see chapter 9); and perhaps some unmarked ones to be engraved. H.H. Rosser, Stationery, Cigars, and Confectionery, 112 N. 4th, Victor, had a single piece engraved "H.H. Rosser" in script, perhaps to commemorate the opening of his business in Victor that year.

Chapter 9

Geo. McMullen ("Mullen"), Shoemaker of Victor

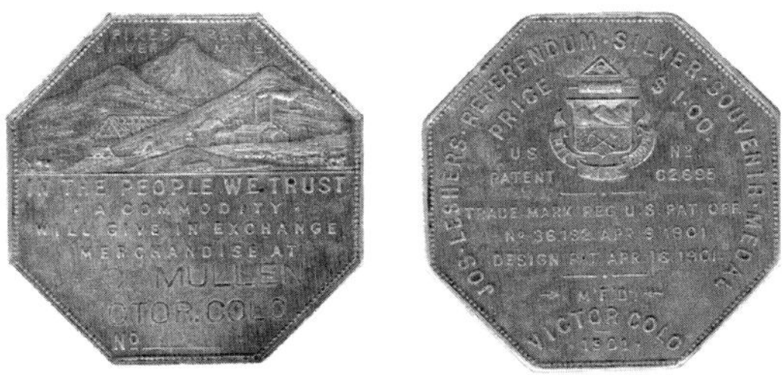

Actual size, 32 mm. *Courtesy of Christopher Marchase.*

Imprint-Type Lesher Dollars are known stamped GEO. MULLEN/ VICTOR, COLO. In 1914, Joseph Lesher told Farran Zerbe that Mullen was a shoemaker, but no person of this name lived in Victor in 1901. However, there was a shoemaker named George McMullen in Victor then. Why McMullen accepted these pieces with his name misspelled is a mystery; none are known with his name given correctly. As mentioned in chapter 8, Joseph Lesher recalled that McMullen had ordered one hundred pieces, but since the numbers known are consistent with a run of just fifty, perhaps he refused delivery of the remainder and they were melted.

George McMullen was, like Sam Cohen, a second-generation American, though his parents were born in Ireland; but unlike Cohen, he failed to make his fortune in Victor.

He was born on August 11, 1861, in Somers Township in rural Tolland County, Connecticut, to William and Harriet McMullen, who emigrated from Northern Ireland in the late 1840s to escape the Irish potato famine. Over one and a half million adults and children departed Ireland for America between 1845 and 1855, and it would seem that the McMullens left soon after they married; in the census of 1850, his mother is shown as having a one-year-old daughter born in the United States, though she was just twenty years old herself. Unlike the persecution of Jews in Russia, however, the potato famine was a great natural disaster, resulting in the deaths of over one million people in five years.

Little George had brown hair and blue eyes. When he was growing up, his father lost the farm in the depression of the 1870s and had to work as a farm laborer, and George was forced to do likewise, as shown by the census of 1880. Clearly, this didn't suit him, and he traveled to California and became a painter. Not seeing any future in that, on October 3, 1882, he enlisted in the U.S. Navy at Mare Island Naval Shipyard, thirty-five miles northeast of San Francisco, with a rank of "Lads" (landsman). (Landsman was the lowest rank, for seamen with less than a year's experience at sea. They performed menial, unskilled work aboard ship—the dirtiest and heaviest tasks—and were forced to endure the harassment of shipmates who outranked them.) A strapping youth of five feet, eleven and one-eighth inches, at that time he was noted as having a "florid" complexion but also knock-knees, a slightly deformed ear and an enlarged tonsil.

Though McMullen was eligible for promotion to ordinary seaman after his three years' service, which took him along the West Coast as far south as Panama, he found that navy life didn't suit him either and was discharged on September 10, 1885, because of Extended Field Service (EFS). He stayed in California and drifted to the former gold rush boomtown of Ophir, by now planted in vineyards and orchards, about ninety miles northeast of Mare Island. George now worked as a waiter, and on Wednesday, September 19, 1888, he registered to vote there.

But he did not stay long in Ophir either, for he was counted in a census of the inhabitants of Tacoma, Pierce County, Washington, on April 1, 1892, working as a laborer. But he was probably just passing through town, since he was not listed in any Tacoma city directory from 1889 through 1893 and must have lived primarily in California, as will be seen.

McMullen now began living alone in a cabin in Butte County, California, northwest of Ophir. This affected his mental health; in early June 1893, he contracted a fever and, in his sickness, deluded himself into thinking that, by filling two bottles with water and placing their necks together, he could "see the sun revolve like the balance wheel of a watch." He considered this a great discovery that would make him "as big a man as Edison."

Others who heard his story were unconvinced, and someone reported him to the authorities. On June 9, 1893, Judge John B. Gray of Butte County ordered him committed to the Stockton State Hospital in Stockton,

California, for monomania. Upon examination the next day, McMullen answered questions "freely" and was "good-natured" but persisted in his delusion. Though he exhibited a muscular tremor in his face and tongue and exaggerated kneejerk reflexes on both legs, he appeared to be healthy other than for his "Acute...paranoia (Wahusian)."

Under the care of Drs. Karsner and Seroiss, he soon recovered and was discharged less than a month later, on August 7, 1893. Though he had no property, he went to San Francisco instead of back to his solitary cabin. Things seem not to have worked out well there either, for he next headed south; he registered to vote in Spadra, Los Angeles County, in October 1894, then a small country town but a station on the Southern Pacific Railroad. (Spadra was annexed to the city of Pomona in 1964.)

Sometime after 1893, he seemingly learned cobbling and moved to bustling Victor, Colorado, to work as a shoemaker, circa 1896–99 (he isn't listed in the *1896 Victor City Directory* and was overlooked in the 1900 directory also, though he owned a house free and clear as of the census of 1900).

McMullen probably repaired the unusual footwear observed by the young Sam Cohen upon arriving in Cripple Creek: "I saw many men wearing mining 'boots' which really were heavy shoes with tops reaching nearly to the knees laced all the way up, with trousers tucked in somewhat like parachute troops of [1940]. But not all of these men were miners." Indeed, a photograph of a member of the Colorado National Guard playing craps during the Western Federation of Miners strike in 1903 clearly shows him wearing gaiters similar to these boots.

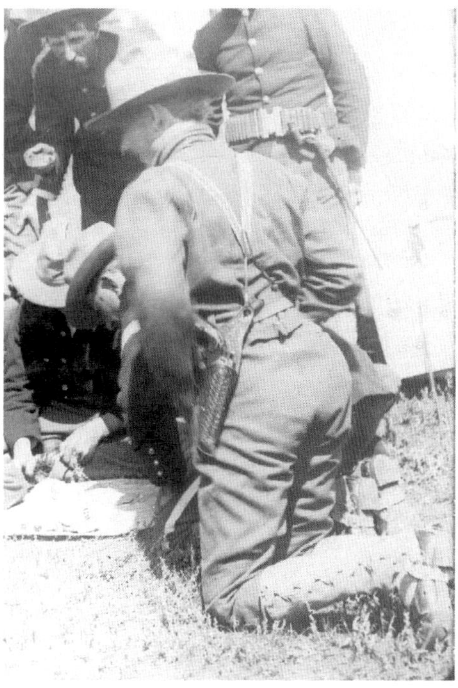

National Guardsman wearing gaiters similar to Cripple Creek miners' boots. *The Denver Public Library, Western History Collection, CHS. X9315 (Yelton & Wisda Photo).*

McMullen's house was located at 507 Victor Avenue (per the Victor city directory for 1902 and 1905; the census of 1900 erroneously shows him at 511 Victor, the same address as Joseph

Lesher), so McMullen was Lesher's neighbor and probably got an earful about his Referendum Dollar scheme. In any case, he ordered a quantity of Lesher Dollars to promote his shoe repairing business and apparently distributed them despite the misspelling of his name.

Like Sam Cohen in 1906, George McMullen could see that Victor's best days were behind it; he last appears in the Victor city directory for 1905. By the time the 1907 city directory came out, he, too, was gone, though unlike Cohen, he had not secured his fortune. But McMullen drifted south and not east, arriving in Yuma, Arizona Territory, by 1910; Yuma is in the far southwestern corner of Arizona, just on the border with California and Mexico. When the census of 1910 was taken, McMullen had his own shoe repair business there but was now renting a house and had taken three other men as lodgers instead of having his own place.

In 1910, Yuma was a small agricultural town, population 2,914, east and south of the Colorado River. Thirteen miles to the northeast lay Laguna Dam, the first dam on the Colorado, completed in 1909. The dam brought an end to steamboat navigation but began the era of irrigation agriculture. So George may have hoped for increasing prosperity in Yuma, particularly with the prospect of Arizona becoming a state; the Arizona Enabling Act was passed by Congress in 1910 and the Constitutional Convention met, but admission was delayed for two years over a clause in the state constitution.

At some point after 1910, however, George gave up shoe repairing and moved to rural San Gorgonio Township, Riverside County, California, about 195 miles northwest of Yuma. There he found work as a hotel porter, as shown in the census of 1920 (name misspelled "Mullen"). He was now living in the hotel as an employee, together with the proprietor and his wife, a waitress and four boarders.

But by then his health was poor. Less than two years later, on January 14, 1922, he was admitted to the National Home for Disabled Volunteer Soldiers, Pacific Branch, in Sawtelle, California (now a district of Los Angeles). Upon admission, he was diagnosed with defective vision, arthritis, "Cardio-Hypertensive-Pyorrhea" (bleeding gums caused by high blood pressure), some obscure ailment and a left inguinal hernia. But he was still erect at almost six feet tall, though he was also said to have a "dark" complexion, probably from his years at sea and in sunny Arizona.

The National Home for Disabled Volunteer Soldiers was established on March 3, 1865, to provide relief for "volunteer officers, soldiers, and seamen" who were "totally disabled" during the Civil War. Over time, eligibility was expanded; in 1884, membership was opened to any honorably discharged soldier or sailor who could not support himself due to a disability. By 1922, there were ten branches coast to coast.

Of these, the Pacific Branch was the most populated during McMullen's stays there. Far from being a single building, it was a miniature town, with many amenities of a fine resort: spacious grounds, a streetcar station on the Pacific Electric Railway, a well-stocked library, a theater, billiards, a chapel with both Protestant and Catholic chaplains, a band, an aviary and a hospital. Fresh fruit and vegetables were served from its own farm.

But the "inmates," as they were called, lived in barracks and took their meals in a mess hall. They were subject to military discipline and had to wear blue uniforms, and these uniforms were surplus from prior wars. Each member was issued a number and assigned to a company, overseen by an officer. Every day they were awakened by a reveille bugle call. Liquor was forbidden.

The regimentation of the National Home did not suit McMullen, and he was "Dropped" on October 18, 1922 (left at his own request or simply went AWOL). Apparently he was able to support himself for the next year, but by the winter of 1924, he was back; he was readmitted on January 8, 1924. This time he stuck it out for over two and a half years, finally being dropped again on June 26, 1926.

He was on his own for yet another year but turned up again on June 29, 1927, to be readmitted for the second time. On this stretch, he lasted another two years or so; he was dropped on April 9, 1930—but he had already walked off before then without being missed, because he was picked up between April 5 and 7 in the census of 1930 in San Bernardino, California, about sixty miles east of the National Home. McMullen was then rooming with another man and was shown as being a "farmer" and on a "farm," despite clearly living in town.

He was readmitted to the National Home, Pacific Branch, for the last time on April 2, 1931. This time, his stay there is uncertain; again, he simply walked off when he chafed at the regimen, apparently so slyly that he was not missed. There is no record of discharge, as if he is still there. Apparently, he lived for a time on a farm in Mira Loma, Riverside County, then a rural area, around 1933; he gave this as his address as of April 1, 1935, in the census of 1940 but must have been mistaken about the year.

After this, McMullen evidently spent the rest of his life in San Bernardino. He lived at 777 Thirteenth Street from 1934 through the November 3 election of 1936 at least, registering as a Democrat in both 1934 and 1936. He seems to have supported himself by doing day labor and repairing shoes, per his voter registrations and a news story in the *San Bernardino County Sun* on January 25, 1936. But he was broke; he had an old account at the Citizens National Trust & Savings Bank in Riverside and, in the winter of 1935, gave grocer William A. Garton a $5 check drawn on it, which was returned for insufficient funds. He was unable to make it good, and Garton swore out a complaint against him on December 11. McMullen was arrested and arraigned on January 24, 1936. Bail was fixed at $1,000 (!), so he probably spent at least several days in jail.

By the November election of 1938, he had moved to a "pensioners home" with nine other elderly men. Initially, he was still working as a cobbler. When the census of 1940 was taken in mid-April, however, he denied having any income from wages or salary in 1939 and said that he was not seeking work because he was unable to work (he was seventy-nine years old). However, he reported receiving at least fifty dollars of income from another source, surely the county Old Age Security Act pension and not Social Security; he did not qualify for a military pension due to his short service. This would have been a maximum of a dollar a day, more likely about twenty-one dollars per month. (But he still claimed to be a shoe cobbler in the *1940 San Bernardino City Directory* and when registering to vote as of August 27, 1940. He had no shop, so he must have repaired shoes as required for another cobbler.)

McMullen once again registered in San Bernardino as a Democrat as of November 3, 1942, giving his occupation as retired. By November 5, 1946, he was living in the San Bernardino County Hospital Old Man's Home. Within fourteen months, he was dead, on January 4, 1948.

George McMullen was born during the Lincoln administration and died during the Truman administration. An uneducated drifter, the high point of his entire life was in 1901 when he beheld fifty shining silver Referendum Dollars with his name (though misspelled) stamped on them. His life went downhill from then, and he died a pauper.

Chapter 10

J.M. Slusher, Grocer and Agent for Cripple Creek

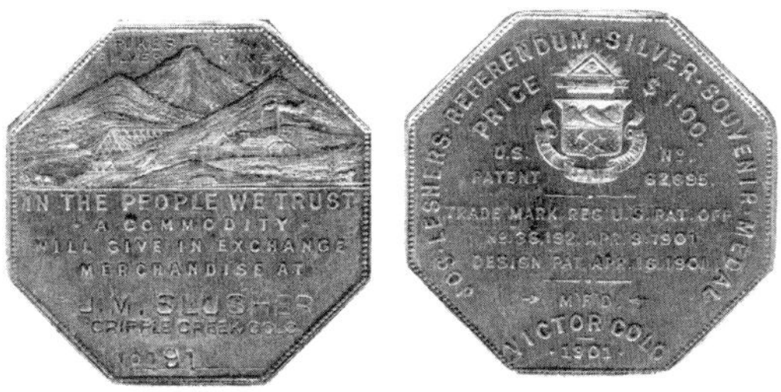

Joseph Lesher appointed grocer James Maurice "J.M." Slusher as his "Exclusive Agent" for sister city Cripple Creek. Slusher's Imprint Type Referendum Dollars are stamped J.M. SLUSHER/ CRIPPLE CREEK, COLO. He ordered fewer than 500, Lesher told Farran Zerbe in 1914, by which time Slusher was deceased, precluding Zerbe from verifying this. Based on the numbers stamped with Slusher's name, Adna Wilde estimated that the total was just 260; the numbers appear to run from 1 through 250 inclusive, plus three in the 540s and 1008, so 260 cannot be far off. However, only 81 are accounted for. But Slusher probably sold an additional 50 to Swedish clothing merchant J.E. Nelson, of Holdrege, Nebraska (see chapter 11), so his total orders were probably in the low 300s.

J.M. Slusher was born in October 1862 on a farm in Malaga Township, Monroe County, Ohio, one of eight children. His father died when he was about four years old, and his mother sold the farm and moved to Logan County in central Illinois. By the time he was twenty-two, J.M. had moved to Lincoln, Nebraska. On Thursday, January 22, 1885, he was married there to Nellie Cochran, an orphan, of Montebello Township in Hancock County, western Illinois, by Methodist Episcopal pastor Dr. Robert N.

Actual size, 32 mm. *Courtesy of Christopher Marchase.*

McKaig. The couple rented rooms in Lincoln, while J.M. worked as a grocery clerk; they were enumerated there on June 8, 1885, when the Nebraska state census was taken.

Two years later, the Slushers moved to the new town of Holdrege, Nebraska, founded in 1883 when the Chicago, Burlington and Quincy Railroad was extended to that point; the first train pulled in on December 2, 1883. At that time, it had a population of two hundred but soon attracted many Swedish settlers, most of them from Illinois. On January 1, 1885, it became the seat of Phelps County. The Slushers soon started a family, and their son James Easson was born on June 10, 1889.

As of 1890, J.M. Slusher was working for Paxton & Gallagher, wholesale grocers of Omaha—one of twenty-one commercial travelers working for this large firm—though continuing to live in Holdrege. He was listed in the Omaha city directory for 1890 as a "trav agt" (traveling agent or traveling salesman). Though he had not lived in Holdrege for over fifteen years, his death out of state was noted with a long obituary in the *Holdrege Progress* on February 29, 1912, beginning, "[He was] one of the most popular traveling men ever living in this city." On May 10, 1890, he bought a fine house at 508 Garfield Street in Holdrege, though he needed three mortgages to cover the cost.

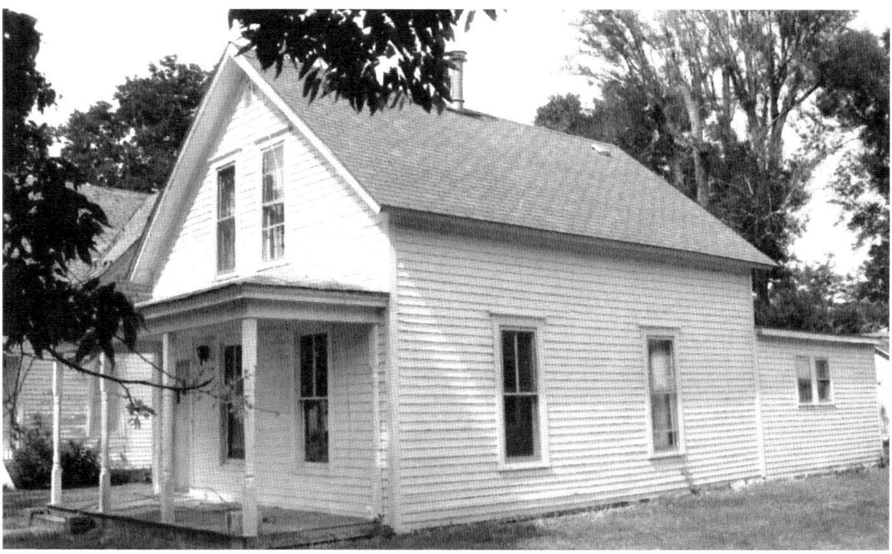

Slusher house in Holdrege, Nebraska. *Courtesy of Jo Ann Knudson.*

J.M. was always ready to share his success with those less fortunate. In November or December 1894, he donated 250 pounds of beans, 50 pounds of tapioca, 50 pounds of rice, two dozen cans of tomatoes and two dozen cans of corn to the Christian Orphan Home in Phelps Center, per the *Holdrege Citizen* of January 10, 1895. Still in existence, though no longer an orphanage, this charity was founded by Reverend Axel Nordin, pastor of the Free Mission Church at Phelps Center, Nebraska, in the summer of 1888. In 1893, the orphans moved into a new two-story building capable of accommodating up to sixty to seventy children.

During 1894, J.M. Slusher was one of the founders of the Nebraska division of the Travellers Protective Association, "Knights of the Grip," and was elected fifth vice-president of the association.

Hearing tales of the vast riches in Cripple Creek, J.M. decided to go into business in Colorado for himself. He left on Sunday night, September 8, 1895, according to the *Holdrege Progress* for September 12, 1895, taking the Chicago, Burlington and Quincy, headed for Pueblo by way of Denver. The next morning, he would have changed to the Denver and Rio Grande to continue on to Pueblo. But finding Cripple Creek more promising, he soon went to Florence via the Denver and Rio Grande and then changed to the narrow-gauge Florence and Cripple Creek Railroad for the last leg.

In no time, J.M. Slusher was "doing a thriving [grocery] business" in Cripple Creek, per the *Holdrege Progress*. He located in the brick and stone Masonic temple at 202 Myers Avenue, at the corner of Myers and Second Street. J.M. soon sent for his family; they left in mid-November 1895. But with winter approaching, they returned two weeks later, leaving him behind. J.M. returned to Holdrege for a week in March 1896, and in June, his wife and son came to visit him. (Their increased prosperity is shown by their eschewing dirty train travel and making a leisurely excursion by horse and covered carriage, together with a local Swedish family. They planned to stop overnight at North Platte, Greeley, Denver and finally Colorado Springs, where J.M. was to meet them and spend a few days.)

The great fires of April 25 and April 29, 1896, left his store and stock untouched by reason of location; his "grocery and provision establishment" was one of only two businesses remaining in the entire city. After the second, and more devastating, fire, he sent two telegrams to his wife in Holdrege to assure her of his safety.

Within two years, Nellie and James Easson moved to Cripple Creek permanently. By August 16, 1897, J.M. had paid off the mortgages on his house in Holdrege, and ten days later, he conveyed it to his wife. Both were

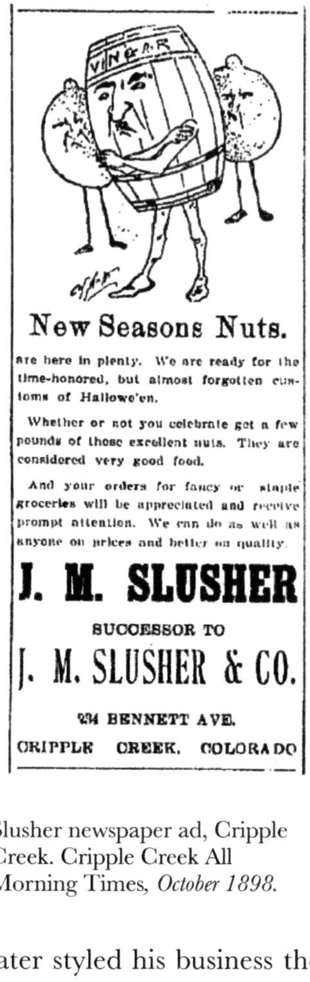

Slusher newspaper ad, Cripple Creek. Cripple Creek All Morning Times, *October 1898.*

then living in El Paso County, Colorado; Teller County, where Cripple Creek is now, was not split from El Paso County until 1899. Finally, on March 17, 1902, the Slushers sold the house at a loss.

On July 18, 1898, their daughter Patty (Pattie) was born in Illinois, among Mrs. Slusher's relatives in Hancock County, probably because J.M. was too busy to help with the baby.

The Cripple Creek city directory for 1896 lists him as James M. Slusher & Co. (James M. Slusher, James Quinn), Grocers, 202 Myers. J.M. himself resided at 129 Warren. He had moved to 234 Bennett Avenue by October 1897, per his display ad in the *Cripple Creek All Morning Times* for October 1897—which stated that he sold only for cash. In the summer of 1898, he acquired his partner's interest and by 1900 was living at 213 North First; he moved his store once again to 165 East Bennett by the time the city directory for 1902–3 was surveyed. There he remained until his death, though he was now living at 206 East Eaton. When the surveyor for the 1907 directory came by, J.M. had added meats. He seems to have later styled his business the C.O.D. Grocery store.

J.M. couldn't resist the temptation to snag some of the immense gold mining profits himself. He incorporated the Commercial Men's Gold Mining and Milling Co. of Cripple Creek on February 12, 1896, with a capital of $1,500,000. The May 10, 1900 issue of *Mining Reporter* mentions that it then owned three gold mines, a lode and had a lease on another property; J.M. Slusher was president and A.B. Olson (misspelled "Olsen" in *Mining Reporter*) secretary. They issued stock certificates of $1 par value, signed by both men. "Commercial Men's has been a favorite with the speculative public during the last thirty days and many thousand shares of this stock have changed hands," reported the *Denver Daily News* of February 22, 1900. At that time, its main office was at 234 East Bennett, in Slusher's grocery store. The

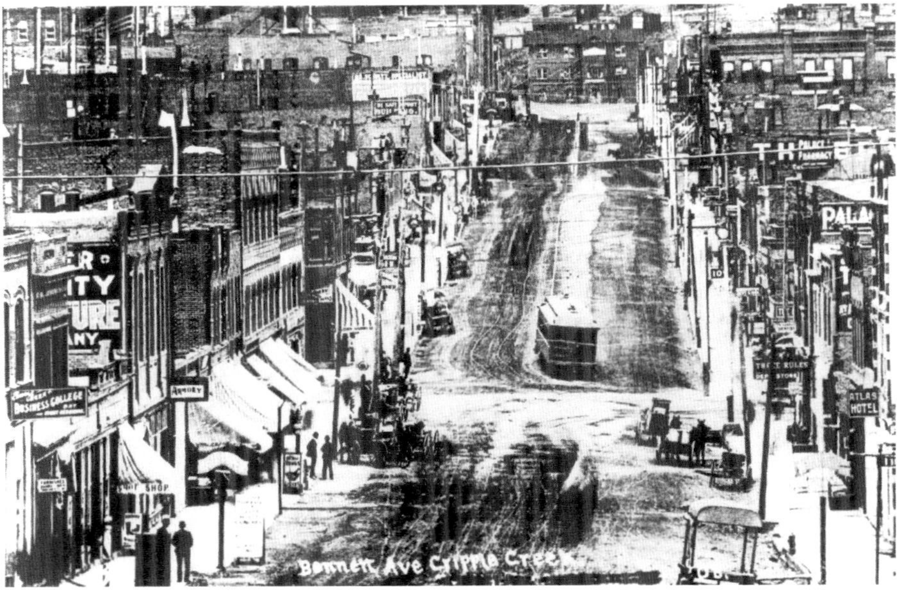

Bennett Avenue, Cripple Creek, circa 1900. J.M. Slusher's grocery was to the left; five wagons are parked in front. *Courtesy of Cripple Creek District Museum.*

January 1901 issue of *Cripple Creek: A Standard Handbook of the Mines and Mining Companies of America's Greatest Gold Camp* notes that the company had moved its headquarters to the Bimetallic Bank in Cripple Creek.

But making money from gold mining was harder than it seemed: one of the company's mines was in receivership, and the "one dollar" value stock traded on the Cripple Creek Stock Exchange for as little as half a cent in 1899. (The 1899 high was twenty-one and a half cents, also a huge loss for anyone who invested in the company at par.) The price of the Commercial Men's Gold Mining and Milling Co. continued to slump in 1901. Bid was 0.8 cents on June 26, but only 0.6 cents on September 5. In a few years, the stock became completely worthless.

And by 1901, he had purchased two vacant building lots on the edge of town, which he mortgaged for $1,000—with interest at 10 percent—on September 1, 1901. He hung on to these until his death, but Cripple Creek never expanded that far, and his widow sold her equity in them for $175.

Fortunately, J.M. had his thriving grocery business to fall back on.

His moving the office of his gold mining company to the Bimetallic Bank is a reminder of the curious situation of a community dependent on gold mining, agitating for bimetallism—the use of both silver and gold jointly as legal tender. The free coinage of silver at a ratio of sixteen to one (by weight) was a key promise of Democratic presidential candidate William Jennings Bryan, but he was defeated in 1896 and 1900. The United States officially went on the monometallic gold standard on March 14, 1900, with the passage of the Gold Standard Act. Nevertheless, many in Colorado still supported the coinage of silver.

Among them was Joseph Lesher, who—as we have seen—produced his own "silver dollars" (actually $1.25) on November 13, 1900. In 1901, he decided to expand beyond Victor and leave a blank space for other issuers; he also reduced the face value to an even dollar for convenience of use. To better distribute them, Lesher appointed five "exclusive agents," of whom J.M. Slusher was the second (name misspelled "J.W. Slusher" on Lesher's card). Slusher was by far the most successful. His were "in circulation" by early May 1901, according to an article in the *Denver Post* on May 3, 1901. Besides those in his own name, J.M. probably took the Lesher Dollar order of J.E. Nelson of Holdrege on a visit to see old friends. An article about the introduction of the Lesher Dollar appeared in the *Holdrege Progress* on November 30, 1900, so Nelson was probably aware of them.

Nelson, a successful clothing merchant, lived in Holdrege from 1888 to 1915, and Slusher would have passed his store, only about two blocks from his house, on his way to the train station for one of his sales trips. No doubt Nelson was acquainted with the gregarious Slusher, who would have had little difficulty in securing the order.

The peak gold production in the Cripple Creek District occurred in 1900; production was disrupted by the great strike of 1902–3 and then by water entering the mines. By 1907, it had dropped below $11 million, and by then many people, Sam Cohen and George McMullen among them, had already departed for greener pastures. What effect this had on J.M.'s grocery business can only be imagined.

But he stuck it out, though his marriage disintegrated. About 1906, J.M. moved out of his house into the store itself, as seen in the *1907 Cripple Creek City Directory* and his suit for divorce, reported in the *Denver Post* for August 6, 1911. One of the parties alleged "cruelty and desertion"—but it was *him*, not her. Nellie, by that time, was somewhat independent, the owner of the Cripple Creek Business College, and the couple had not lived together for the past five years, he said.

In the winter of 1912, he became sick and was taken to the Sisters of Mercy Hospital in Cripple Creek, where after five days he succumbed to pneumonia on February 22, 1912, his divorce not yet final. He was only forty-nine. His gray granite tombstone can be seen in Mount Pisgah Cemetery, Cripple Creek.

J.M. had provided for his family by taking out a large life insurance policy and never changed the beneficiary, so $5,000 was paid on April 10, 1912; this was wise because his widow, Nellie, did not have an easy time after his sudden death. The house at 206 East Eaton, which was being rented, was foreclosed. She began teaching school and soon rose to Teller County superintendent of schools. About 1920, she and her daughter moved to Colorado Springs.

James M. Slusher's estate was not settled until March 6, 1920, over eight years after he died. Perhaps Nellie, the administrix, was hoping to collect money owed to her husband or sell some mining stock. But the receipts she assembled list no stock sales at all and no large collections. In total, she was able to gather just $963.90 from cash in bank, store accounts, store fixtures, secondhand furniture, "unknown thru mail," "sale of junk," etc. After final expenses, there remained only $726.10. Colorado law at that time provided for a "widow's allowance" of $2,000 for maintenance of the family during the period that the estate was being settled, and since the value of the estate was less than this, the court awarded the entire remainder to her.

The *Cripple Creek Times* published Slusher's obituary on February 23, 1912:

> *The deceased was jovial and had many friends in the district. He was always known as a man with a big heart and when he had an opportunity to do a friend a good turn, he was always willing to accommodate him as far as he was able to do so. He was one of the best known men in the district and made many friends through the medium of his congenial nature. In the sixteen years he lived here he gave many thousands of dollars worth of groceries to the needy.*

When his estate was settled, among his effects was found a single "souvenir coin," no doubt one of his personal Lesher Dollars; evidently, he had sold all the remaining ones and retained just one as a keepsake. Even in 1920, it was a valuable collectible; it realized two dollars.

Chapter 11

J.E. Nelson, Dry Goods, Holdrege, Nebraska

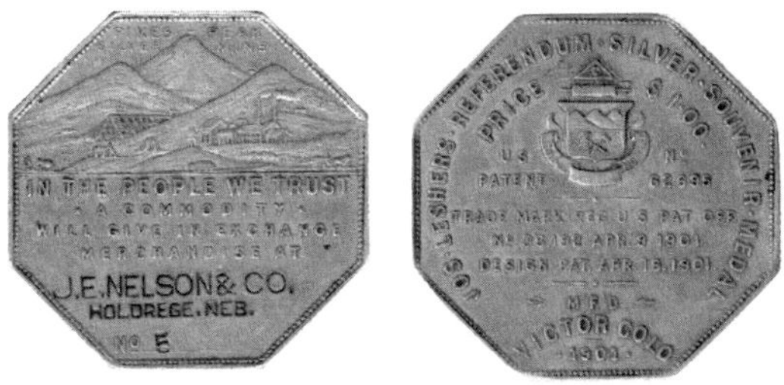

As mentioned in the previous chapter, Cripple Creek agent J.M. Slusher probably sold Imprint-Type Lesher dollars to his former fellow Holdrege resident J.E. Nelson, to be shipped by Joseph Lesher from Victor. In 1914, Joseph Lesher remembered selling Lesher Dollars to two clothiers, one in Grand Junction (see chapter 17), but could not then recall the location or name of the other. He told Farran Zerbe that they had been supplied in blank, so Nelson must have had them stamped locally. Numbers from 5 to 41 are recorded for pieces stamped J.E. NELSON & CO./ HOLDREGE, NEB., so presumably Nelson ordered fifty pieces. His was the only business outside Colorado to use Lesher Dollars. But who was J.E. Nelson?

John E. Nelson was a first-generation American, born on January 1, 1865, in Jönköping County, Sweden, to John and his second wife, Maria Agusta (Mary) Nelson. He was one of five children. Probably the Nelson family would have remained in Sweden but for the great famine of 1866–68. By 1868, John Nelson had had enough and immigrated to the United States, to Rockford, in northern Illinois, a popular destination for immigrating Swedes in the 1860s. He bought passage to his final destination from a Swedish ticket broker, a common practice at the time.

Actual size, 32 mm. *Courtesy of Christopher Marchase.*

So John Nelson and his family—his wife, three-year-old John E. and August, only two—sailed to England, boarded a ship to New York, took a train to Chicago and finally changed to the Chicago and North Western Railroad for the final leg to Rockford. The Nelson family lived in Rockford for two years, and their third child, a daughter Josephine, was born there on April 23, 1870.

Later that year, John investigated the new village of Maywood in Proviso Township, Cook County. But John had not been able to do better than find work as a watchman in a Maywood factory (as of the census of 1880), and his two older sons had dropped out of school and were working too.

This was surely not the wonderful life in America that John had hoped for when he left Sweden. About this time, he heard about the rich farmland of Nebraska, perhaps from Union Pacific Railroad land agents Leander or Frank Hallgren, who persuaded many families in Illinois to homestead in Kearney and Phelps Counties. So—at age sixty-five—John Nelson pulled up stakes and moved his family once again, settling in Kearney County, Nebraska, in 1881.

In 1880, the census found John E. already working as a clerk in a store in Proviso Township, Illinois, at fifteen, but he moved to Nebraska with the rest of his family and started over, living in Lincoln Township, Kearney County. As of the 1885 Nebraska state census, he was boarding with three other young Swedish men, all employed as clerks.

Three years later, he went to work for Sol. G. Mayer in Holdrege, and within two months, Mayer had taken him in as a partner for a new clothing store. Mayer & Nelson, children's and men's clothing, opened on April 1, 1888, at the corner of East Avenue and Hayden Street (renamed Fourth Avenue in November 1906). The partnership consisted of S. & C. Mayer, Sol. G. Mayer and John E. Nelson.

On their first anniversary, April 1, 1889, Mayer & Nelson held a delayed grand opening. A marching band played, and every visitor got a souvenir: "The ladies received an exquisite bouquet of violets, and the gents each a pocket book and the statement that if they would trade with this firm they would always have money in their purses." Per the *Holdrege Citizen* of April 4, 1889, 1,700 souvenirs were given away on April 1 and another 400 the next day.

But on May 1, 1891, Mayer and Nelson dissolved their partnership "by mutual consent." Almost immediately, a new firm—now with John E. Nelson as the senior partner—replaced it, likely at the same location. In partnership with Charles C. Little, Nelson announced the grand opening of Nelson & Little, successor to Mayer & Nelson, on May 11, 1891. Just a year later, though, Nelson & Little took out a three-year lease for the lower story and basement of the building on the northeast corner of East and Hayden, apparently the location of their enlarged store for the balance of the partnership.

Nelson & Little had bigger plans and around 1894 opened a branch store in Seneca, Kansas, about two hundred miles southeast of Holdrege. While Little remained in Holdrege, Nelson began shuttling between the two stores, spending much of his time in Seneca. Finally, the partners gave up on the branch store, selling it to Bardley & Hart in the summer of 1896.

Despite this setback, the business of Nelson & Little was quite profitable. By 1894, John E. Nelson owned land near his father's property in Logan Township, Nebraska, and as of August 1 of that year, he bought the former building of the defunct Farmers State Bank of Holdrege, which had voluntarily closed in December 1892—"except the Bank counters and [vault] doors." Purchased as an investment, this lot was later incorporated into his final and greatest store. A lifelong bachelor, Nelson saved his money and eventually bought out his partner, probably in the summer of 1900.

Meanwhile, entrepreneur John W. Trammell—who for $20,000 in the late 1880s purchased the concession to manage all the "Eating Houses" on the Burlington and Missouri Railroad from Lincoln, Nebraska, to Akron, Colorado—needed a new source of income when the B&M introduced dining cars in 1889. He invested in the Farmers State Bank of Holdrege, but the bank was not successful and closed voluntarily, with no loss and no creditors, and as mentioned, the building was later sold to John E. Nelson. A few years later, Trammell began constructing a large brick building on this site, the "Trammell Block." John E. Nelson apparently had an interest in this project, since he owned one of the lots it was on, and planned to relocate his clothing store there.

So Nelson, now sole proprietor, advertised a "Removal Mark Down Sale" in the *Holdrege Progress* on August 14, 1900, announcing that "THE TIME has arrived to unload our entire stock as near as possible and make a clean sweep prior to our removal to our new quarters in the Trammel [*sic*] block which is now nearing completion." Completion was not as near as he supposed, but at last the Nelson Clothing Co. held its grand opening on October 26, 1900, on the southwest corner of East Avenue and Hayden Street, diagonally across from the former store. This location was twice the size of the old store, having two stories plus a basement. With expanded space, Nelson "added one new line to their business, that of ladies' fur capes

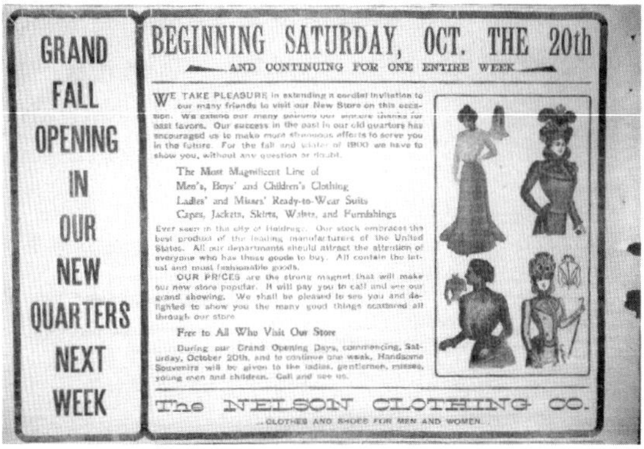

Left: Ad announcing Nelson's grand opening, October 1900. Holdrege Progress, *October 20, 1900.*

Below: Nelson Clothing Co. store as it appeared 1903–6. *Courtesy of Jo Ann Knudson.*

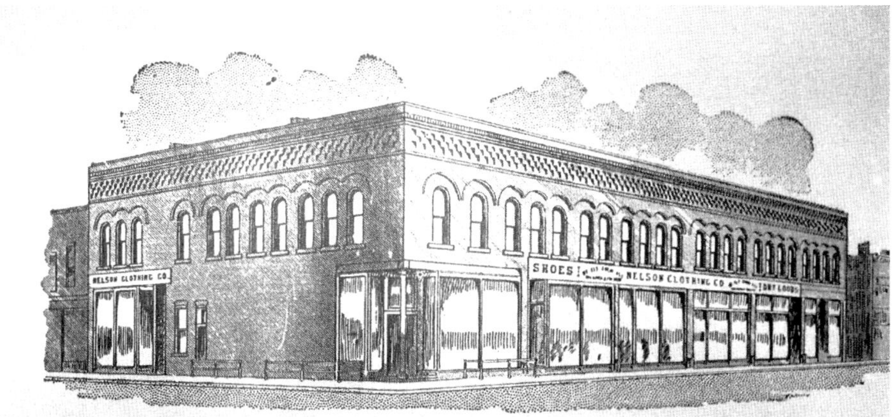

and cloaks, skirts, shirt waists, ladies ready to wear clothing of all kinds and a full line of ladies furnishing goods," reported a Holdrege newspaper.

For two days, the four-piece Venuto Bros. harp orchestra of Omaha played, and "[d]uring opening week each caller—lady, gentleman, boy or girl—[was] presented with a souvenir…whether the recipients buy a cent's worth of goods or not." The *Holdrege Weekly Progress* of November 2, 1900, characterized the souvenirs as "little."

The Nelson Clothing Co. was a heavy newspaper advertiser in the early 1900s. John E. Nelson referred to this in an interview published in *Dry Goods Reporter* on January 3, 1903. He also explained the business plan that had made him so successful: "Our model in the organization of our store is the Nebraska Clothing Co., with their main store at Omaha. Apart from this store we believe we have the most complete stock of ready-made goods to be found in the state." Nelson was strongly focused on customer preferences: "Our experience regarding help is that male help is much more satisfactory in a ladies' furnishing goods department than female help. In fact we employ throughout the store gentlemen salespeople almost entirely. In the ladies' ready-made garment department we have both gentlemen and ladies, but I have found that even the women prefer gentlemen to wait on them." (Modern antidiscrimination laws would probably prevent this!)

On May 4, 1903, Nelson sold the former Farmers State Bank land back to John W. Trammell at a slight profit, and Trammell began altering the Trammell Block to accommodate yet another doubling of Nelson's space, from a frontage of fifty feet to one of one hundred feet; this was accomplished by cutting two arches through to a space equal in size to the original. On October 22, 1903, Nelson held his fourth grand opening; a three-piece orchestra from Denver played five hours per day for the duration of the event. If any souvenirs were distributed, they were not mentioned in the newspaper report.

John E. Nelson's optimism that he had room to grow his sales and needed the additional space proved correct. After his last expansion, he added a stock of dry goods, according to an interview published in *Dry Goods Reporter* on March 12, 1904. Through the rest of the nineteen oughts, he promoted his business as "The Big Double Store of Little Prices."

Nelson was a genius at marketing: for his annual clearance sale of winter goods on January 1, 1904, he decided to make over his high-class store to look like a "job lots joint," he told the interviewer for *Dry Goods Reporter*. He crowded the aisles and counters with bins and boxes to resemble a big city bargain outlet, and "[w]hen we had our boxes and bins ready we dumped into them our merchandise just the same as they do in the bargain stores. We put prices on these goods....There was no effort made by us to keep the merchandise in presentable condition. In fact, we did exactly the opposite.... We unrolled goods and tangled them up as much as possible."

The next step was to promote the sale, and Nelson covered the front of the store with signs and "went to the livery stables and hired livery men to drive into the country with our advertisements and deliver them to every farm house along the road. We told them to drive as far as they could and back in one day and do the distributing thoroughly."

The result of this risky experiment was gratifying: "People crowded into the aisles....The eagerness with which the people hunted through the special offerings was particularly...pleasing to us." He increased sales for January by 200 percent!

Even more innovative was his "hayrack loads of women" publicity stunt on February 3, 1906. Three weeks before, Nelson offered prizes to the three

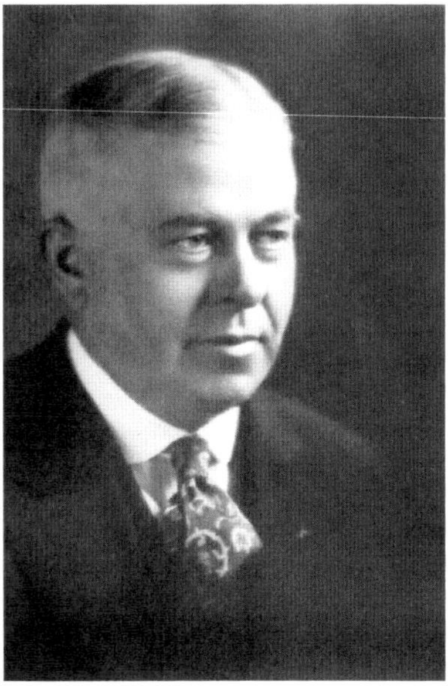

John E. Nelson. *Courtesy of William M. Nelson, Jr.*

persons who could bring the biggest loads of women to his store, according to the *Holdrege Citizen* of February 9. The winner, who received twenty dollars in cash, had a hayrack with fifty-six women on it. The second prize of ten dollars went to a man who brought twenty-four women to town, and the third, five dollars, for a load of sixteen women. And those who couldn't get in the loads came some other way. The result was that, for an investment of thirty-five dollars plus a photographer, Nelson packed his store with six hundred female shoppers!

Later that year, he began styling his business as the Nelson Company and incorporated it in October 1907 with a capital of $75,000. In 1909, R.G. Dun rated its credit "Good," with a net worth of $50,000 to $75,000. Nelson invested his growing profits in land, including recreational property. On Saturday night, June 19, 1909, he "tendered the employees of his store the usual annual banquet....About thirty-nine places were set...the main course being black bass, which Mr. Nelson and Mr. S.F. Nelson [no relation] had personally secured from the privately stocked lake belonging to Mr. Nelson in the western part of the state, the day previous...remarks were heard to the effect that 'John Nelson certainly treats his clerks right,'" according to the *Holdrege Citizen* of June 24, 1909.

Unfortunately, 1909 was the zenith of success for the Nelson Company. For several years beginning in 1910, the Holdrege area experienced poor crops and business conditions; the company's farmer customers were expected to settle their accounts after the harvest, but with poor returns, many could not.

By 1914, Nelson had fallen behind in payments to creditors to the point that the Nelson Company was forced into involuntary bankruptcy. Nelson assigned the assets of the Nelson Company to trustees on June 30, 1914. On December 19, 1914, Nelson announced the end of his business in the newspaper: "It didn't work out as we expected and so this sad announcement. For it is sad to bid farewell to a community of long friends and associates." His final sale was announced in the *Holdrege Progress* on January 7, 1915:

"Quitting Business. The end of The Nelson Co.…The Sale must be brought to an end—To end expenses; to end rent; to end clerk hire; to end advertising. JOIN THE CROWDS AT THE NELSON CO." The remaining merchandise was sold at auction the next month.

After the store closed, John E. Nelson got a second chance at success: early in 1916, Julius Pizer, owner of the Leader store in North Platte, "suffered a physical break-down from overwork" and gave up active management, and Nelson was brought in to run the business. On March 30, 1916, it was incorporated under the name of the Leader Mercantile Co., with a capital of $30,000 and Julius Pizer, president; J.E. Nelson, vice-president, general manager and treasurer; and Anna Pizer, secretary. The store was to carry a general stock of dry goods, with the business managed by Nelson.

He arrived in North Platte on July 6 to begin inventory, and on August 20, 1916, he left "for Chicago and other eastern points to purchase goods," per the *North Platte Semi-Weekly Tribune* of August 22.

While Nelson relied, as other stores did, on many small front-page ads in the *North Platte Semi-Weekly Tribune* resembling news items, he also tried various promotions to boost business. He staged "Dutch Auction" sales in 1920 and 1921, dropping prices "a dollar every day" (February 20, 1920) and "$2.00 each day" (January 25 and February 1, 1921); he passed out encased cents in 1920 (token catalog TC-184376; encased); and he topped these stunts with a precursor of Black Friday, May 2, 1922—one-dollar discount certificates to the first ten adults to enter the store after the sale began for the first five days and five gallons of gas free for anyone spending twenty-five dollars or more, in appreciation of them "coming a long distance."

Despite these heroic efforts, the Leader Mercantile Co. was out of business by the time the *1925 North Platte City Directory* was surveyed. Nelson took a series of jobs in Nebraska in the late 1920s, but by 1935, he was living at the Maryland Hotel in St. Louis, as mentioned in the census of 1940. In 1940, he was still at the same address, working forty hours per week at age seventy-five, selling office supplies on his own account. He died there on February 14, 1945, still working as an office supply salesman at eighty. He is buried in Hastings, Nebraska, next to some of his siblings.

Since Holdrege is far from Pikes Peak, what prompted John E. Nelson to order Lesher Dollars? Dr. Philip W. Whiteley investigated this question, and in *The Numismatic Scrapbook Magazine* for December 1958, he wrote, "I succeeded in locating a man, who in his younger days, worked as a clerk for this [Nelson] clothing firm, in 1901. This gentleman says that the Nelson Leshers were given to customers during a formal opening of the store when the firm moved to new quarters, in the Trammel [*sic*] Block, Holdrege, Nebraska." The implication is that they were given out in 1901, but as we have seen, Nelson had *four* grand openings: April 1, 1889; May 11, 1891; October 26, 1900; and October 22, 1903, the latter two both in the Trammell Block. The first three are prior to the minting of *any* Lesher Dollars, and the fourth is over two years after the release of the Imprint Type issued by Nelson.

This discrepancy troubled Charles A. Stowers, who published "The Riddle of the Nebraska Lesher" in *The Numismatist* in January 1991. He reprinted a Nelson Clothing Company ad from the *Holdrege Weekly Progress* of October 12, 1900, mentioning free souvenirs (though he failed to realize that the grand opening was postponed from Monday, October 22, to Friday, October 26, as can be seen from the November 2, 1900 article he reprinted from the *Weekly Progress*). Even so, Nelson's grand opening was over two weeks before the release of the first Lesher Dollar.

As Sherlock Holmes remarked in *The Sign of the Four*, "When you have eliminated the impossible, whatever remains, *however improbable*, must be the truth." Clearly Dr. Whiteley's informant confused the grand opening of 1900 with that of 1903; it was, after all, two years after he left employment as a clerk—and over half a century before being contacted by Dr. Whiteley.

Also, the contemporary press account of the 1903 grand opening makes no mention of anything of value given to customers, as Stowers noted. And were Nelson to have handed these out to all comers, he would have required thousands, not 50 (he had passed out 2,100 souvenirs at his first grand opening, fourteen years before).

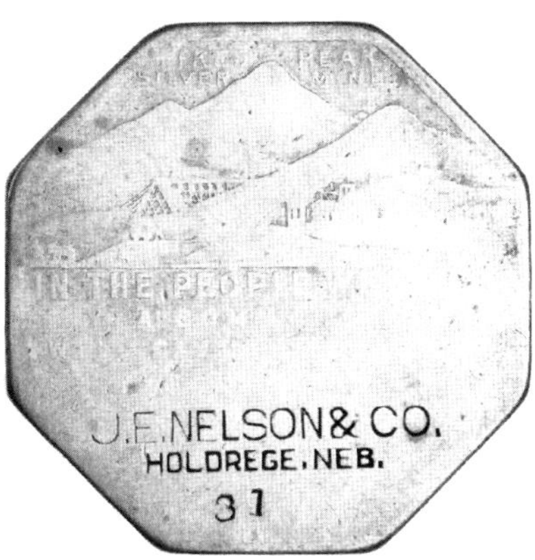

J.E. Nelson Lesher Dollar discovery piece, used as a pocket piece. Actual size, 32 mm. *Courtesy of American Numismatic Society, New York.*

So, if they were in fact distributed at the 1903 grand opening, who received them? From the *Holdrege Citizen* account of John Nelson's "usual annual banquet" for his employees, June 24, 1909, we learn that "about thirty-nine places were set." If Nelson had the same number of employees six years earlier, he would have needed about thirty-nine pieces for them, plus three more for the orchestra, or around forty-two—leaving about eight leftovers for future use out of an order of fifty. So the most probable explanation is that these silver "dollars" stamped with the company name were mementos presented personally to everyone who assisted with the 1903 grand opening.

This appears to be confirmed by their rarity in the market: allowing for hoards reported by Dr. Whiteley, Nelson's Lesher Dollars are the rarest of all the Imprint Types, with just 16 percent of the issue recorded today. They were so tightly held that they remained unknown to collectors for nearly thirty years. On August 26, 1932, stamp and coin dealer J.G. Anderson of Denver wrote to Farran Zerbe, then curator of the Chase Bank Collection of Moneys of the World, offering one he had "bought the other Day" that was so extremely worn that it was obviously a pocket piece. Zerbe bought this discovery piece, but for his personal collection, not for the bank, though he donated it to the American Numismatic Society in 1947 with the rest of his second collection.

Had they been given out in change like the others, we should expect that they would have been known to collectors as early as the rest. Rather, they seem to have been preserved as treasured heirlooms, saved in memory of a merchant who "certainly treats his clerks right."

Chapter 12

BOYD PARK, JEWELER AND AGENT FOR DENVER

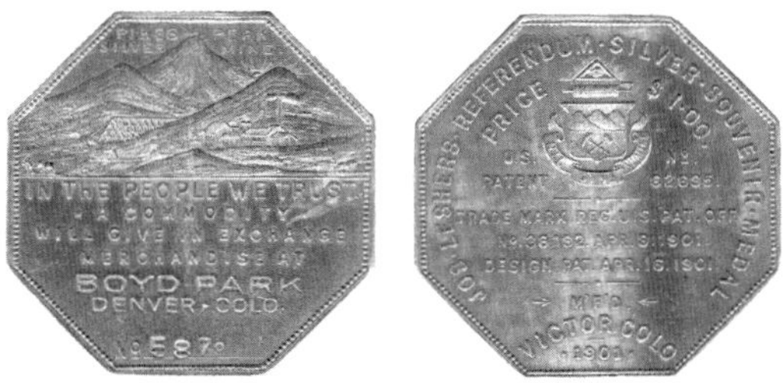

For his Denver "exclusive agent," Joseph Lesher appointed the city's leading jeweler, Boyd Park. His Lesher Dollars are stamped BOYD PARK/ DENVER, COLO.

(Note: Two biographical sketches of Boyd Park were published during his lifetime: "Boyd Park," in *Biographical Record of Salt Lake City and Vicinity*, 1902, and "Boyd Park," in *Sketches of the Inter-Mountain States 1847–1909*, 1909. Unfortunately, they contradict each other on many points. The information presented here is believed to be correct, as far as can be determined.)

Boyd Park was another first-generation American and self-made man, born on December 28, 1837, in Elderslie, Renfrewshire (western Scotland), the son of Alexander Park and his wife, Margaret Stephenson Park. According to his son almost seventy years later in *Sketches of the Inter-Mountain States*, Alexander Park "conducted a silk weaving establishment at Ellerslee [Elderslie], Scotland." But Alexander Park was gone from the scene by about 1840, and Margaret moved to nearby Bridge of Weir, where Boyd attended school, though he had to drop out to work in the silk mills.

Struggling to support her family, Margaret sent eleven-year-old Boyd Park to America alone; he arrived in New York City on June 28, 1849, on

Actual size, 32 mm. *Courtesy of Christopher Marchase.*

the *Herald*, and settled in Troy, New York, probably with relatives. There he received the rest of his education. In 1852, he became an apprentice at the local firm of William L. Adams, jewelers, where he excelled, working there as a jeweler until the spring of 1862. Park then moved to Poultney, in Rutland County, Vermont, where he formed a partnership in the jewelry business with Jervis Joslin under the firm name of Joslin & Park.

As the Civil War drew to a close, the partners decided to relocate to the West. In the spring of 1865, they packed up their tools and machinery and shipped them to St. Joseph, Missouri, where they outfitted for the dangerous trip on the Overland Trail. Using ox teams to haul their baggage, they walked across the plains to Denver, arriving late in the fall, according to the *Denver Post* of March 15, 1910, and April 9, 1913, and *Biographical Record of Salt Lake City*.

At this time, Denver was very much a frontier town of only 3,500 or fewer inhabitants, devastated in turn by fire, flooding, grasshoppers and Indian attacks on supply trains. With the end of the Civil War, however, the city began to grow again. Joslin & Park opened their jewelry store at 38 Larimer Street in May 1866; their first ad appeared in the *Rocky Mountain News* on July 5, 1866, offering Swiss watches, diamonds, jewelry and "Silver Ware."

In 1867, the transcontinental Union Pacific Railroad chose a route through Cheyenne, Dakota Territory, a blow to Denver's hopes as a transportation hub. The city responded with a plan to link Denver and Cheyenne by rail; ground was broken in 1868, and the first train from Cheyenne arrived on June 24, 1870. Joslin & Park lost no time in taking advantage of these developments, opening a branch in Cheyenne on December 17, 1867, to be managed by Boyd Park, per the *Cheyenne Leader* of that date. They hadn't been open a year, though, when a fire swept through half a city block in Cheyenne (now in Wyoming Territory) on October 7, 1868; their loss was $5,000, including their building and some of their stock, the *Rocky Mountain News* reported. But they purchased "a large and substantial frame building and moved it on to the site of their former building which was destroyed by fire," according to the *Cheyenne Daily Evening Leader* of October 20, 1868, and quickly recovered.

Besides retail sales, they manufactured gold watch chains and moss agate jewelry, according to the *Report of the Commissioner of the General Land Office to the Secretary of the Interior for the Year 1872*. Soon they closed their store in Denver and consolidated all their Colorado business in Cheyenne.

Boyd Park opened another Joslin & Park establishment in 1871 in Salt Lake City.

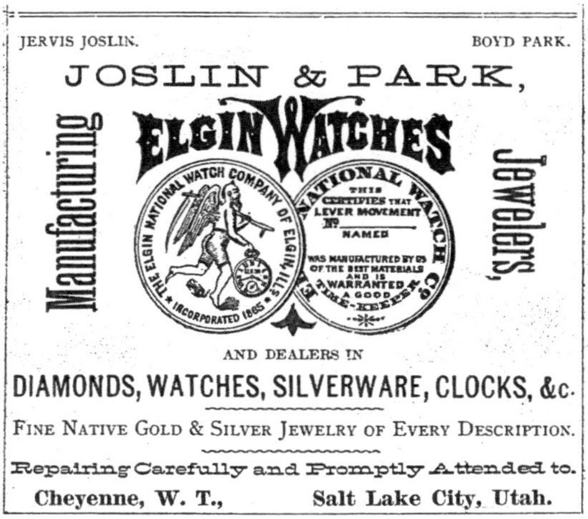

Joslin & Park ad in *Utah Directory and Gazetteer for 1879–80* (Salt Lake City, 1879).

In 1879, Jervis Joslin headed for silver mining boomtown Leadville, Colorado, to open yet another branch. The Cheyenne store was closed in the spring of 1880, and the Colorado business consolidated in Leadville, where Joslin & Park was the largest jewelry store in town. Early in 1887, the Leadville store was closed, and Joslin moved back to Denver. There he opened a new store in the center of town, this time in the prestigious Tabor Grand Opera House Block, at the corner of Sixteenth and Curtis Streets.

In the meantime, in January 1869, Boyd Park, "while living in Cheyenne...returned to Poultney, Vermont, where he was married to Miss Jane E. Culver, a native of that state. By this union two children [were] born, Colonel Samuel Culver Park and Margaret B. Park," according to the *Biographical Record of Salt Lake City*. Jane, known as Jenny, became ill in 1892 and left in September for New York City for her health, reported the *Deseret Evening News* of February 4, 1893, "but instead of becoming better she grew worse. Last night her son, Sam Park, received a telegram urging him to come at once if he wished to see his mother alive. He left on this morning's train. Shortly after his departure a dispatch conveyed the sad intelligence that she had died at 10:30 this morning." She was only forty-nine. Boyd Park never remarried.

All these stores used the Joslin & Park name until a year after Joslin died in Denver on January 4, 1899. In March 1900, Boyd Park's son, Samuel Culver Park (then associated with his father in the business), purchased Joslin's interest in both stores from his estate, and the firm name was changed to Boyd Park, successor to Joslin & Park, according to the *Salt Lake City Daily Tribune* of March 24, 1900.

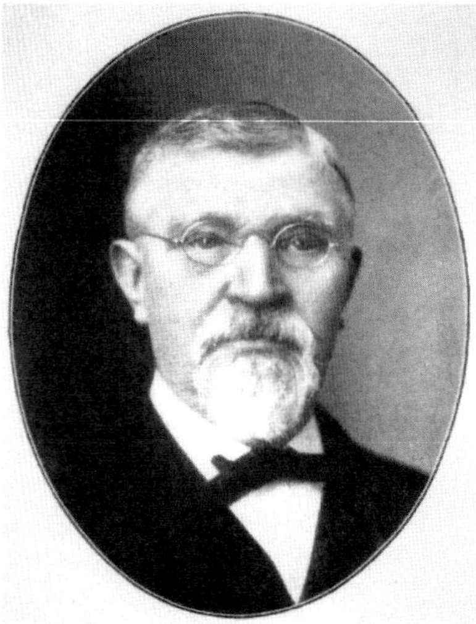

Boyd Park. *Courtesy of Jo Ann Knudson.*

After buying out his late partner's interest, Boyd Park remained in Salt Lake City until his death, though after 1903 Samuel Culver Park became manager of the Salt Lake City branch. However, Boyd Park frequently visited the Denver store, where he was often seen checking up on things from an easy chair on the rear balcony, as noted in the *Denver Post* on April 9, 1913. Besides the retail stores in Salt Lake City and Denver, Park's manufacturing department was the largest in Colorado and, indeed, "one of the largest jewelry establishments in the entire West," according to the *Denver Post*, September 24, 1899, and *Biographical Record of Salt Lake City*.

In *The Mercantile Agency Reference Book* for July 1906, the Boyd Park Jewelry Co. was rated C+1 (pecuniary strength $125,000 to $200,000, General Credit High).

On May 1, 1910, the lease of Boyd Park's Denver store expired, and being then seventy-four years old, he decided to retire rather than seek a new location. He announced that his entire stock, said to be worth $200,000, would be cleared out at discounts of 25 to 50 percent. Less than three years later, on April 8, 1913, he succumbed to heart failure while on a visit to his daughter in California. On April 13, he was laid to rest in Mount Olivet Cemetery in Salt Lake City, under a Masonic escort.

Besides his jewelry business, Boyd Park was the first president of the territorial Bank of Commerce in November 1890, according to the *Deseret Evening News* of November 7, 1890, and later a director. Like so many others in the West, he caught "silver fever." He was, at various times, a director or officer of the Free Silver Mining Company (1880), the Queen of the Hills Mining Company (1884), the Triumph Mining Company (1885–87) and others; he was also president of the NL Live Stock Company of Cheyenne, Wyoming Territory (1889). Park was a Mason of "the highest degree," a Knight Templar and a Mystic Shriner. He served on the Salt Lake City Library Board for several years, though he never held public office.

In 1901, Denver—"the Queen City of the Plains"—was the capital of Colorado and the largest city in the state, with a population of 175,000. In

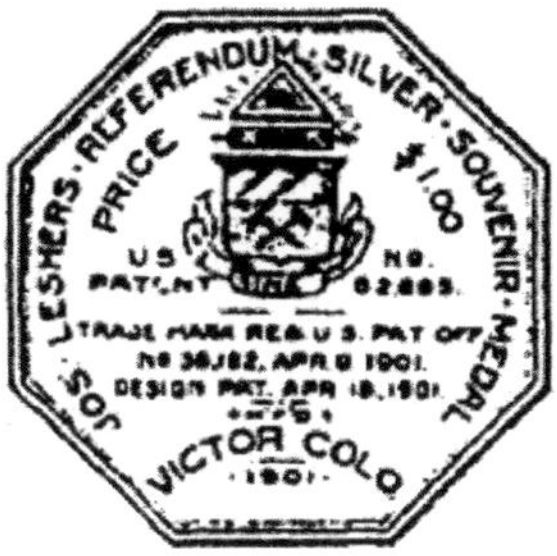

Face of the Dollar

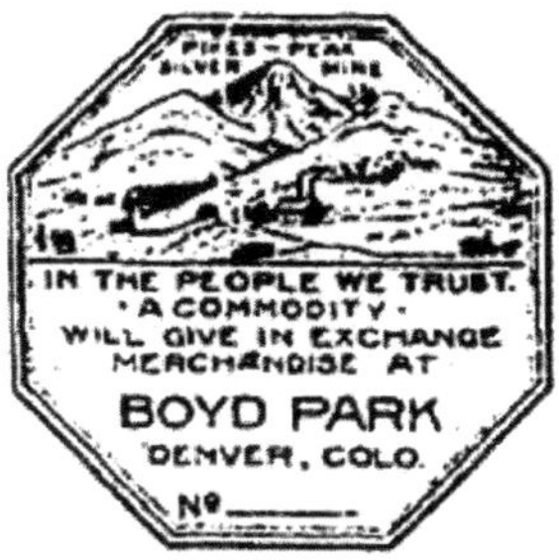

The Reverse Side.

Illustration of Boyd Park Lesher Dollar. Denver Post, *May 3, 1901.*

the center of town stood the Tabor Grand Opera House Block, which included the Boyd Park Jewelry Co. "The interior is very handsomely furnished in hard wood and heavy plate glass show cases," reported the *Denver Post* on September 24, 1899. At that time, Park had about twenty employees, managed by Frank P. Allen.

The *Denver Post* of May 3, 1901, reported, "The Lesher referendum dollar is now in circulation. One firm in Denver and another firm in Cripple Creek will accept it payment for merchandise. The Denver firm is Boyd Park....The dollar contains more silver than the American dollar." Illustrated was an unnumbered example of Boyd Park's Lesher Dollar. Zerbe later wrote in the *American Journal of Numismatics* that "Denver people remember seeing quantities, hundreds they say, heaped in Park's store window."

Be that as it may, Wilde supposed that Park had only 150 pieces stamped; he had recorded numbers running from 502 to 648, but at least 15 unnumbered pieces are known, so a total of 200 or more is not unreasonable. In 1914, Lesher told Zerbe that Park sold between 500 and 1,000 pieces. Since Park "was Lesher's distributing agent [in Denver] for several months," he may have sold some to other known users for stamping with their names (though this would not add up to several hundred) or distributed others entirely blank. Zerbe mentioned that Park "is said to have had an interest in this remainder [of the blank Imprint Type] and it is supposed that they were reduced to bullion; however, this is not certain."

Boyd Park was an unusual Lesher Dollar agent because he was a Republican, according to the *Biographical Record of Salt Lake City*, and thus a supporter of the gold standard and opposed to the free coinage of silver. He seems to have been indifferent to the silver controversy that motivated their issue because he treated them as merchandise, not currency; when sales slacked off after a few months, he closed them out!

Chapter 13

C.W. Thomas, an Agent Who Vanished

Like Charley the MTA rider, "he never returned, And his fate is still unlearn'd." Joseph Lesher appointed jeweler C.W. Thomas as his "exclusive agent" for Florence, Colorado; he was supplied with his orders in blank. But Thomas apparently never had any pieces stamped with his name and must have sold them as received, perhaps engraving a name on them as a memento (see chapter 18, H. Stein).

Florence was a jumping-off point for the Cripple Creek gold district. Founded in 1870 as a railroad depot, it boomed in 1881 when black gold—oil—was discovered and fields developed. The first brick building on Main Street was built in 1887, the year Florence was incorporated with a population of 450. In 1890, gold was discovered at Cripple Creek; by 1892, the mines were connected to Florence by a road, and on July 4, 1894, the narrow-gauge Florence and Cripple Creek Railroad across Phantom Canyon opened to carry the ore to the railhead in Florence.

At about 5:00 a.m. on Monday, June 23, 1902, C.W. Thomas left his Florence home "in a cheerful humor" before breakfast, telling his wife that he was going for an hour's walk. He was never seen again.

When he had still not returned by 10:00 a.m., she became alarmed and went to the jewelry store, which she found still closed. After his wife reported him missing, volunteers sprang into action. Over one hundred men and boys scoured the hills and ravines around Florence all day and into the evening, and the nearby mountains were searched on horseback at the direction of the marshal, to no avail; "foul play" was suspected.

Mrs. Thomas told the authorities that she feared that "he had possibly made away with himself as he [had] been despondent for several days and was brooding more or less over a contemplated change he intended to make in the location of his business." She denied any domestic problems and asserted that his accounts were all straight.

Bloodhounds were brought from the penitentiary at Canon City that evening. They "easily" followed his trail "to a point on the bank of the [Arkansas] river about a mile and three-quarters below town. Here the trail was lost completely." Surprised at this, the handlers gave the dogs a fresh scent, with the same result—they went straight to the riverbank. It was then supposed that he had drowned himself in the river, and a party of twenty Odd Fellows dragged it for his body from the Pikes Peak bridge to half a mile below the county bridge, a distance of two miles, with no result. (A body *was* seen floating in the Arkansas River in July, but it wasn't his.)

A report of June 24 that he had been found in Victor "in a demented state" was soon discredited.

On Wednesday, June 25, the Independent Order of Odd Fellows offered a $50 reward for the discovery of their past grand master and grand warden, and Mrs. Thomas topped that on June 28 with the offer of a $100 reward "for the return of her husband alive or dead, or for information leading to his recovery." Circulars printed free at the *Florence Citizen* office were scattered about Florence and vicinity. Thomas's office safe was opened on Wednesday afternoon at his wife's request, and "all the missing man's money and jewelry was found intact."

But apparently there were suspicions even then that there was more to the story than had been revealed: as early as June 25, the Florence police sent circulars describing Thomas to southern Colorado towns, and pictures of him were forwarded to their counterparts in Denver, Colorado Springs, Pueblo, Leadville and other Colorado cities the following day. An officer was even sent to Canon City on horseback to determine whether he had been seen there. It was supposed by some that, "while temporarily insane, [he] wandered off and was either drowned in the river or met his death in the hills." However, "[m]any people are inclined to believe that he has left this part of the country and will probably be picked up in some [*sic*] of the nearby cities," according to the *Colorado Springs Gazette*.

The Odd Fellows—baffled by the lack of results—selected a committee that met with Mrs. Thomas on Thursday but came away no wiser. She now could not say whether her husband left home at 5:00 a.m. or at midnight the night before and denied that he owned a straw hat, though "many people" in town saw him wearing one. (This question came up because a straw hat was found floating in the river.) Some began to believe that Thomas left town deliberately and Mrs. Thomas was hiding something.

After the committee made its report, the Odd Fellows, suspecting "some crooked work," withdrew their reward offer on Saturday, June 28, "for good reasons": information had surfaced that "before he left Thomas donned a new suit of clothes, a new hat and new shoes." While this hardly seems suspicious, "it was also learned today that Thomas was agent for a Colorado Springs company [National Home Investment Association, see below] and that a few days before he had collected a large sum of money. This money has not been received by the company's officials yet and Thomas had drawn all but a very little money from his bank account here." It was insinuated that his wife "does not seem to be feeling much worried and it is generally believed that she is concealing something that she knows about the affair."

In "A Card" published in the *Florence Daily Tribune* on July 1, 1902, Mrs. Thomas protested that these and other innuendos being circulated about her husband were not true. She denied that she and C.W. had a heated quarrel on the Sunday before he disappeared and that he told her "that if he ever left her it would be useless for her to look for him." She also said that he had not slipped out before daylight and that he was not wearing a new suit of clothes, new shirt and new pair of shoes but "wore the same shoes and suit he was accustomed to wear about the store. He did not even put on his new hat and gloves as was his custom when he contemplated a trip."

She also denied not notifying the police or his relatives in the East and explained her declining to join in the search because she did not like to go away from the store. Above all, she professed to be shocked that "persons who [insinuated that she was not 'wholly in the dark regarding the matter'] have pretended to be my friends, and...should slander me to a newspaper reporter behind my back."

Following this defense, however, the *Daily Tribune* refused to retract any of its statements, which it said "were simply made on what the management had reason to believe to be good authority, and up to this time the *Tribune* has no reason to recall any of [them]." It added hopefully, "Time alone will reveal the truth." But the *Silver Cliff Rustler* was less optimistic: the July 2, 1902 issue stated, "It is now generally believed that he is not dead but has deliberately left the country [*sic*] and has used every precaution to elude his pursuers. His whereabouts may never be discovered."

His disappearance certainly cut short Thomas's career as a Lesher Dollar agent, even though Lesher was still distributing cards listing him as late as 1903. Prior to this episode, C.W. (Charles) Thomas seemed perfectly normal. He was born in Ohio in October 1864 and married Cora R. Moore of Nebraska on January 26, 1893, in Colorado; their daughter, Julia Thomas, was born about six months later. For several years prior to 1900, he had his own jewelry store in Florence, at 103 West Main Street, and lived with his wife and daughter in his own house. On December 20, 1900, he announced that H.W. Williams, a jeweler from Washington, D.C., had accepted employment with him.

Nothing seemed out of the ordinary at first in the months preceding his disappearance; his advertising was typical for the time, though somewhat apologetic and defensive. He sold his jewelry for cash only and argued in his advertising against selling on credit. In the *Florence Citizen* for October 25, 1901, he admitted that he did not have the largest jewelry store in Fremont County, nor the only one in Florence, but boasted that "WE HAVE some of the finest GOODS ever presented to the buying public....No old goods to work off on you, everything new." On November 15, he announced that a chance at a forty-dollar diamond and opal ring would be "given away with every purchase, large or small."

But business must have been slow, because he advertised a home loan scheme in the *Florence Citizen* on March 2, 1902. Offered by the National Home Investment Association of Colorado Springs, organized on January 2, 1902, this plan would loan money to buy a house as follows:

A	\$500	house	\$5.50	per	mo.	for	100	mos.
A	\$1000	"	\$11.00	"	"	"	100	"
A	\$1500	"	\$16.50	"	"	"	100	"
A	\$2000	"	\$22.00	"	"	"	100	"

This equates to an annual interest rate of just 2.3 percent, far below the usual mortgage rate of the time of about 6 to 10 percent and even under the U.S. Treasury rate of over 3 percent, so an upfront payment was required to secure one of these loans, from which Mr. Thomas would take his commission as agent. The National Home Investment Association advertised this plan in other Colorado newspapers as late as April and May 1902, but seemingly, prospects were leery, and the scheme failed.

Finally, in June 1902, C.W. Thomas ran a large display ad announcing "REMOVAL SALE! 25 & 35 per cent off on any article in the House. I have decided to take the vacant room in the Van Nest block. And in order to raise a little money for the next ten days I will offer you any article in my store at 25 to 35 per cent Reduction on Regular prices." This ad, running three times per week, actually appeared in the same issue as the notice of his wife's offering $100 reward for his return!

In July, hope for Thomas's reappearance having ended, his jewelry stock was inventoried at $2,446.00 "at list price with no reduction on account of time of purchase." But at Thomas's discount sale, the value was but $1,834.50 (25 percent) or even $1,589.90 (35 percent). "The indebtedness is reported as some $1,800," showing that Thomas was essentially insolvent. An assignment was made to the Denver wholesale and manufacturing jewelers Chas. Wathen & Co. (name misspelled "Whehen" in the *Florence Citizen* of July 19, 1902); evidently, Thomas acquired much or all of his stock from them on credit.

Chapter 14

D.W. Klein, Agent and Pueblo Saloonkeeper

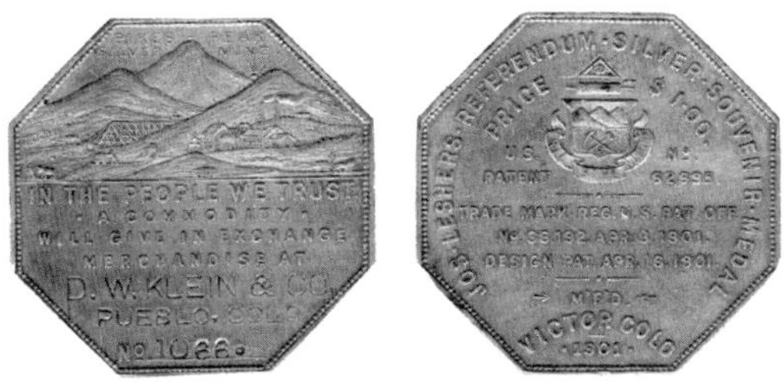

The third wave of Jewish immigration to the United States began in 1881. Most came from Russia, but all of eastern Europe was represented. Among those seeking a better life was David W. Klein, apparently born on May 28, 1865, probably in Morva, in the Nagy-Mihály District, Zemplén County, Hungary (now in Slovakia) [correcting the "Legene Mihaly" of his 1912 passport application to Nagy-Mihály, plus the Hungarian census of 1869 for Zemplén County]. An "old friend" of Joseph Lesher, he was appointed "exclusive agent" for Pueblo, Colorado, in 1901. He issued Lesher Dollars stamped D.W. KLEIN & CO./ PUEBLO, COLO.

Like a roly-poly toy, David Klein absorbed several hard blows in his life that would have felled a lesser man but always righted himself and persevered.

He was residing in Sáros County, Hungary (also in Slovakia now), when he made the decision to leave. At that time, he had no skills and declared himself to be a "laborer" when he boarded the *Polaria* in Hamburg on November 1, 1882, claiming to be eighteen years old. He arrived in New York on November 23, still pretending to be eighteen.

Of his time in New York nothing is known, except that he met and married his first wife there in the late 1880s; their daughter Lillian was born in New

Actual size, 32 mm. *Courtesy of Christopher Marchase.*

York in January 1889. Later that year, the family moved to Colorado, perhaps for his wife's health, if she was suffering from consumption (tuberculosis). When the *May 1890 Denver City Directory* was surveyed, David W. Klein was shown as a clerk, working for F. Kohn.

But not long afterward, Mrs. Klein died, leaving him with an infant to care for. Klein acted quickly, and on August 20, 1891, he was united in marriage to Mollie Berkowitz by Orthodox Rabbi Solomon Arager of Congregation Ohava Emuno, according to the *Rocky Mountain News* of the same date. Mollie, a recent arrival to Denver, was born in Hungary in August 1866 (as "Mali") and arrived in New York, by herself, on June 11, 1883, age sixteen. The following June, Klein's second child, Sadie J. Klein, was born to the newlyweds.

The Denver city directory published in May 1894 showed David W. Klein trying to support his family as a "pedler." But not long afterward, he gave this up and moved to booming Victor. The first we hear of him is as a bartender in the Combination Saloon there, as listed in the Cripple Creek directory for 1897. (This saloon, in downtown Victor, was owned by John Klein, apparently no relation.) No doubt David Klein met Joseph Lesher around this time. Murray S. Klein, David and Mollie's second child and David's third, was born on October 23, 1897.

By June 1900, David was sufficiently successful to open his own saloon, as we learn from the *1900 Cripple Creek City Directory* and the Victor census of 1900, taken on June 8. At that time, Klein's family was living with him in a rooming house in Victor with four other roomers, including fellow saloonkeeper Bernard G. Greenwood. In June 1900, however, Klein moved from Victor to Pueblo, about seventy miles southeast by train, to open a saloon there. The county seat of Pueblo County, Pueblo then had a population of about fifty thousand and was the second largest city in Colorado; it also enjoyed mild winters, since it was at five thousand feet lower elevation than Victor. (David W. Klein was counted a second time in the census of 1900, on June 13, as a single roomer in Pueblo.) The Pueblo city directory for 1900 gave the address of his saloon as 201 South Union Avenue.

In the summer of 1901, Klein obliged his friend Joseph Lesher by issuing Lesher Dollars in the name of D.W. Klein & Co., Bernard Greenwood apparently being the "& Co." if indeed there was one. Only one was ever presented for redemption, the rest entering circulation in Pueblo or saved as souvenirs. Later that year, the name of the saloon at 201 South Union was formally changed to Klein and Greenwood, per the Pueblo city directory for 1901–2.

Though he had left Victor, gold fever had not left David Klein; on November 26, 1901, Klein and a partner, Adolph Stark, conveyed mining deeds to a claim for "nominal" consideration and received an undivided half interest in a second claim in the Cripple Creek District from another speculator, according to the *Colorado Springs Gazette* of the next day. Klein and Stark did not make enough from this investment to quit their day jobs, but they remained friends for many years thereafter.

The Klein and Greenwood saloon, however, continued to prosper through 1906; in July of that year, R.G. Dun & Co. rated their general credit as Fair and pecuniary strength as $2,000 to $3,000, but business was clearly picking up. In 1904, David's fourth child, Jeanette T. Klein, was born.

The Pueblo city directory for 1907 showed that the saloon at 201 South Union had now been replaced by the Gold Label Bar at 229 North Union Avenue, still owned by Klein and Greenwood. Two years later, the Pueblo directory revealed that a second company had been formed—Klein, Greenwood & Co.—in addition to Klein and Greenwood, the third partner being Adolph Stark. The new partnership opened a second saloon at 180 North Union Avenue, while the Gold Label Bar continued as before. However, the new venture was apparently not a success, for it is absent from the *1910 Pueblo City Directory*. But Klein and Stark remained friends.

The Gold Label Bar name was retained through the 1911 directory. In the 1910 census, David Klein is listed as a "wholesale" liquor merchant, though the bar itself was certainly retailing; perhaps this is an error by the enumerator, or maybe Klein had added wholesaling by this time. The 1912 directory shows the name of the saloon at 229 North Union Avenue reverting to Klein and Greenwood, with Adolph Stark taken in as a partner. Stark remained as a partner in 1913 but was dropped by the time the 1914 directory was surveyed. After renting various locations in Pueblo, by early 1911 Klein could now afford to buy a house for his family at 107 Veta Avenue.

In another sign of his growing prosperity, David W. Klein became a naturalized citizen of the United States on June 11, 1912, and applied for a passport the next day, stating that he intended to travel abroad for up to five months. His identity was vouched for by old friend Adolph Stark. The passport clerk recorded that Klein stood five feet seven and a half inches tall and had gray hair and a mustache, with gray eyes, a high forehead, a straight nose and a "dark" complexion.

Then disaster struck: Colorado enacted Prohibition, which took effect on January 1, 1916. Klein and Greenwood was out of business.

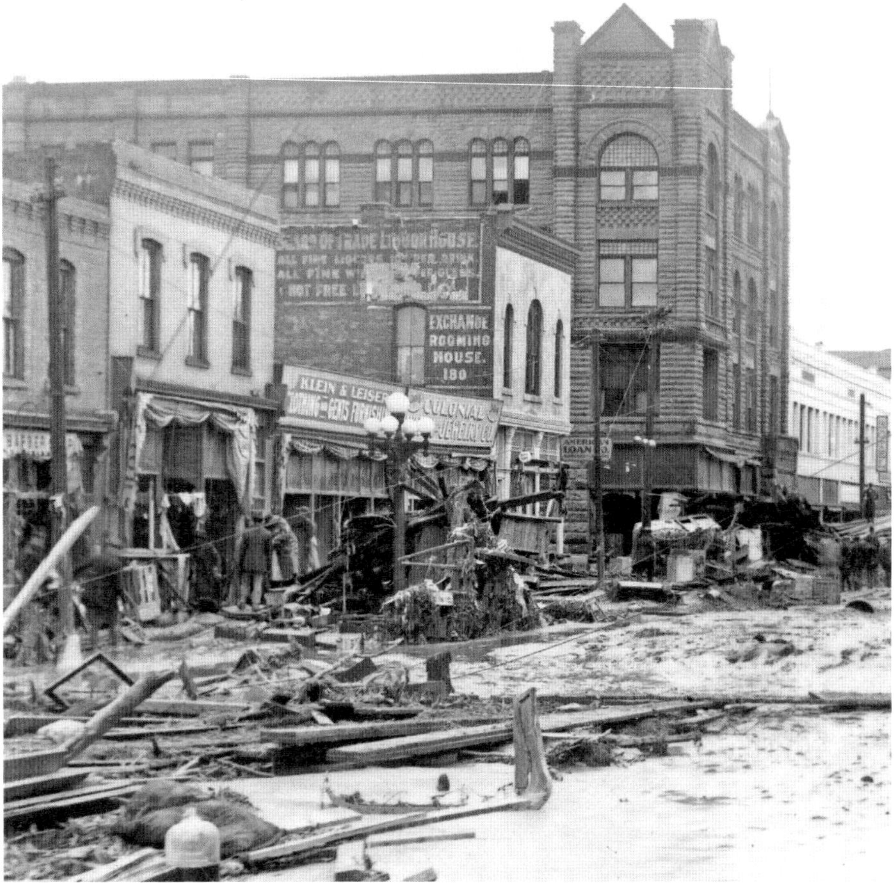

North Union Avenue looking southwest following 1921 Pueblo flood; store of Klein and Leiser in center of picture. *Courtesy of Pueblo City County Library District, Special Collections, Rawlings Library: ph-p-295-06-002jpg-Photos [Ralph Taylor photo], cropped with permission.*

Trying to adjust to life without liquor, Klein tried selling but by 1917 had formed a partnership with grocer Joseph Leiser, as Klein & Leiser, for a clothing business. Their store was located at 306 North Union Avenue in Pueblo. In the carelessly recorded census of 1920, "Dave Klien" was recorded as a "Salesman" who worked for a wage or salary, though it would appear from his business style that he was co-proprietor. By this time, he owned his house free and clear.

This new prosperity was not to last. On June 3, 1921, the Arkansas and Fountain Rivers, which join in Pueblo, overflowed in a disastrous flood that took 1,500 lives and caused $20 million in damages. Almost all of downtown Pueblo, including the store of Klein & Leiser, was destroyed.

The *1921 Pueblo City Directory*, issued after the disaster, listed David and "Molly" still living at 107 Veta but with no occupation. Evidently, Klein was trying to collect his insurance and assess the possibility of rebuilding his business.

With no partner, he opened a grocery at 120 South Union, as shown in the Pueblo directory for 1923, but soon gave this up and by 1925 had moved away. Where he spent the next few years isn't known, but the census of 1930 found him renting a home in Inglewood, California, the proprietor of a fur shop there, at age sixty-five.

Mollie died in Los Angeles on June 15, 1932; David never remarried. He followed her in death on November 19, 1941, and was buried in the Garden of Shalom section of Hollywood Memorial Cemetery (now Hollywood Forever Cemetery), Hollywood, California, with a Star of David marker. He lies not far from the last resting place of many of filmland's most famous names, from Rudolph Valentino to Mickey Rooney.

In 1914, Klein told Farran Zerbe that he had "experimented" with Lesher Dollars in 1901 because he was "an old friend" of Joseph Lesher. "He had three hundred, paid Lesher 85 cents apiece for them, used them in change and trade at $1.00, and only one ever came back for cash redemption," Zerbe wrote. However, Lesher Dollar accumulator Jean Maunovry, who lived in Denver at the time, said that they had only limited circulation in Pueblo.

Adna Wilde, writing in 1978, doubted Klein's account. He thought that only one hundred were issued because the range of serial numbers recorded spanned only from 1036 to 1075, plus 971, based on twelve recorded serial numbers. Two more stamped pieces have surfaced since then, but the range has not been extended. But Dr. Whiteley knew of a hoard of seventeen pieces, serial numbers not recorded, that has not surfaced (perhaps once owned by Edward Broadbent Morgan; see chapter 15). In addition, an example (serial no. 7) with the legend engraved and not stamped appeared at auction on September 26, 2007. The size and spacing are the same as for the stamped pieces; it may be a pattern to show how the stamp should look.

Was Klein's recollection faulty? A total of 300 pieces is not impossible. Perhaps many were supplied to him blank: the blank Imprint Type is known with serial numbers from 1 to 47 (but no 7) and 1002 to 1049. In addition to these two groups of 50, about another 18 are known unnumbered, plus 439. Very likely Klein did not purchase the whole 300 at once but in batches of 100 or 50. If so, he may well have received 150 stamped with his name (numbered 951–1100), followed by 100 numbered but blank (lost or broken stamp?) and finally a batch of 50 with neither stamp nor number. He was the only issuer in Pueblo, so they would probably have been accepted even without his name.

Chapter 15

W.C. Alexander, Jeweler of Salida

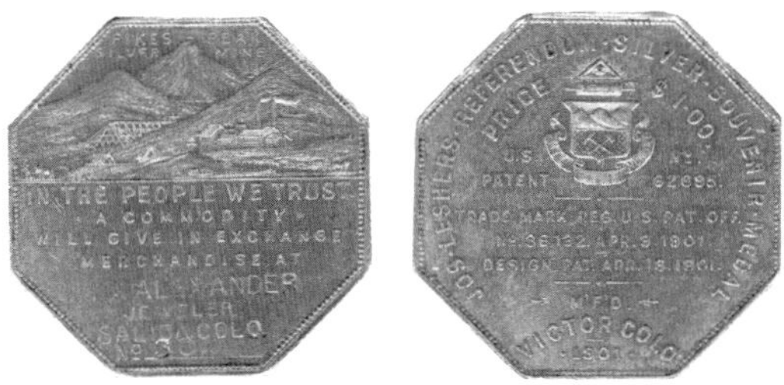

Though Joseph Lesher preferred his customers to purchase from one of his "exclusive agents," he allowed Salida, Colorado jeweler William Calvin Alexander to buy directly. Alexander ordered fifty Lesher Referendum Dollars from Lesher in March 1902, paying forty dollars for them, he wrote Farran Zerbe in 1918. They were stamped W.C. ALEXANDER./ JEWELER/SALIDA, COLO. (the second A in SALIDA is broken so that it resembles an inverted V) and numbered from 1 to 50. As of then he had none on hand, he told Zerbe. Today only thirteen are known, none numbered higher than 37. As with Klein, however, Dr. Whiteley knew of a hoard of six pieces, serial numbers not recorded, that has not surfaced.

Unlike many other Lesher Dollar issuers, Alexander was no newcomer to America; he later became a member of the Sons of the American Revolution. He was born on December 23, 1871, in La Grange, Fayette County, Texas, the son of Thaddeus Thompson Alexander, a civil engineer who surveyed much of Texas. In 1880, he was attending school in Austin.

By mid-1883, the Alexander family had moved to San Antonio, with Thaddeus employed by the Galveston, Harrisburg and San Antonio Railway as a civil engineer. About 1885, William began working for local watchmaker

Actual size, 32 mm. *Courtesy of Christopher Marchase.*

and jeweler Eliezer Hertzberg, probably after school and on Saturdays. But after his father died on September 14, 1886, he dropped out of school at fifteen and took a job as a clerk for Jessop M. Bell, a leading San Antonio watchmaker and jeweler. He continued working for Bell until the mid-1890s, learning the business and deciding on jewelry as a career.

Since many jewelers at the time were branching out into eyeglasses, Alexander left Bell's employ and began the study of optics at the "Optical College of Chicago" (little more than a diploma mill), receiving the degree of "Doctor of Ophthalmology" in 1897. The next year, he moved to Houston to work as an optician for J.L. Mitchell, a manufacturing and retail jeweler at 402 Main, but soon moved across the street to the store of Louis Lechenger at 403 Main. Alexander did not remain in Houston long, however, for two years later, he was employed as a salesman for Joseph Linz & Bro., wholesale and retail jewelers of Dallas; in short order, he was promoted to manager of their retail department.

Though he had improved his status by these changes, Alexander was dissatisfied and felt that he was ready to go into business for himself, if he could find the right location. Throughout his moves, his mother had remained in San Antonio. After a visit to her in 1901, he decided to scout out possibilities instead of returning directly to Dallas. He took the Atchison, Topeka and Santa Fe Railway as far north as La Junta or Trinidad, Colorado, and switched to the Denver and Rio Grande, heading west toward the mining regions.

He never arrived. The *Salida Mail* of April 18, 1902, explained that he "was so well pleased with Salida and the possibilities of a bright future that he decided to locate permanently." At that time, Salida was a thriving mining and railroad center with a population of 3,722; the Cripple Creek strikes led to a wave of prospecting and new towns nearby, and there was talk of construction of a smelter. But of more interest to Alexander was the fact that Salida was a division point for the Denver and Rio Grande, with a large roundhouse, car shops and even an official Rio Grande hospital.

The *Mail* continued, "He at once instituted negotiations for the purchase of P.T. Shirkey's watch and jewelry business. The negotiations were successful and Mr. Alexander…took possession of the store." Wm. C. Alexander opened for business in Salida on August 16, 1901, with P.T. Shirkey handling watch and jewelry repair for a time before his death.

Alexander moved swiftly to improve the business, offering the just-purchased Shirkey stock at one-third off for a week to make room for new stock—expected to arrive shortly—according to his ad in the *Mail* of that

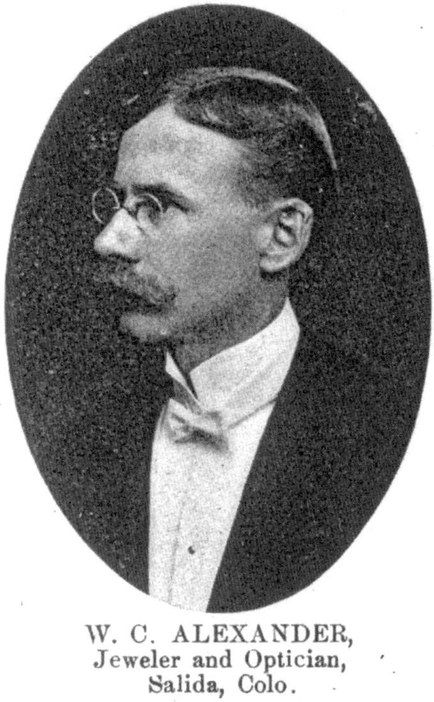

Right: W.C. Alexander, early 1900s. *Judy Micklich, Salida Museum.*

Below: Interior of W.C. Alexander's jewelry store, early 1900s, showing a pair of spittoons. *Judy Micklich, Salida Museum.*

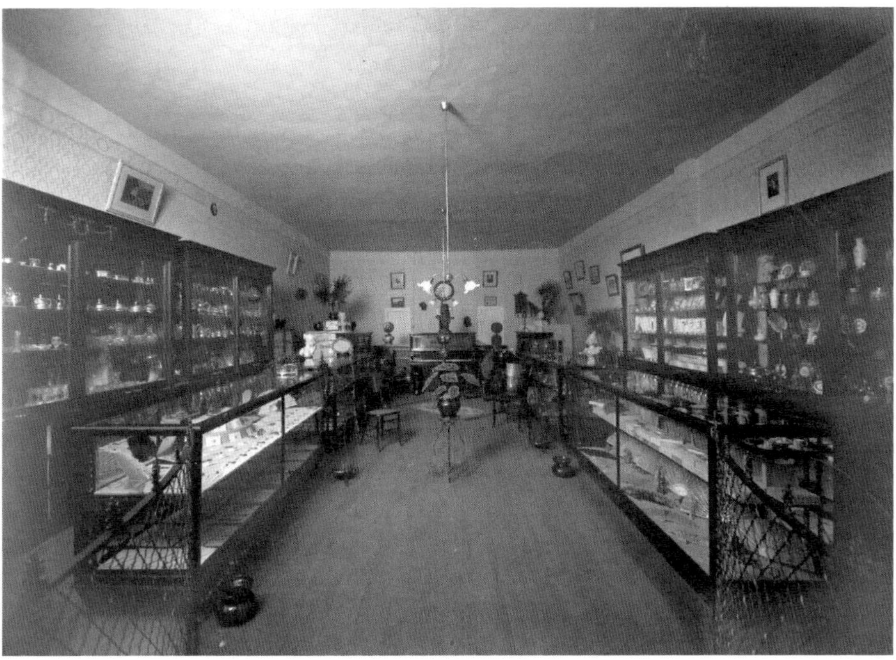

date. The store was to be completely redecorated: new paint, new wallpaper and new mahogany showcases. Even so, it presented quite a contrast to the luxurious emporium of Boyd Park in Denver: a narrow, dimly lit space with a wood floor, equipped with a pair of spittoons.

In those days, it was extremely critical for every railroad employee to have the correct time, to ensure maximum utilization of track and equipment—and to avoid collisions. All employees were required to own special railroad watches and have them inspected once a week to ensure that they did not deviate more than thirty seconds (approximately four seconds per day). As a division point, Salida had many customers for such watches, and Alexander did a good business with them.

In the March 4, 1902 issue of the *Salida Mail*, he ran an eight-column ad across the top of the page, headed "R.R. MEN ATTENTION!" to promote his stock of watches conforming to the new watch standard of the Denver and Rio Grande. In it, he claimed to have sold a "great number of high grade movements…during the past two weeks." Later that month, he ordered fifty Lesher Referendum Dollars, an odd purchase for him since he was a Republican and not a Free Silver advocate. But according to his wife in an article in the *Salida Mountain Mail* on April 30, 1969, he used them in trade for a time. He did not advertise them, though, and never reordered.

Like many retailers, Alexander saw the advantage of having pretty girls as sales clerks. In 1902, he hired Miss Jennie Valdez, who handled bookkeeping as well as sales. And in the holiday season of 1905, he added Miss Harriet Lucinda Wright, age twenty-four, who had come to Colorado for her health. While Jennie worked for Alexander for many years, he fell in love with Harriet and married her on July 2, 1907, at her mother's home in New Castle, Indiana. For their honeymoon, he took her to the Jamestown Exposition—after first stopping at the Knights Templar conclave in Saratoga Springs and the Elks convention in Philadelphia!

To boost his lucrative railroad watch business, Alexander joined the Brotherhood of Railroad Trainmen and was listed in its monthly publication, *The Railroad Trainmen's Journal*, in January 1907. He also tried to have himself appointed time inspector for the Denver and Rio Grande, hoping to compel trainmen to visit his store periodically to have their watches checked for accuracy, but was unsuccessful. In the fall of 1907, he began issuing attractive annual catalogues, going through seven editions.

In 1910, he added drugs to his store by purchasing the drug business of G.W. Armstrong and later consolidated it with his jewelry and optician business, dividing his store with drugs on the right and jewelry on the left. As of 1921, there were five drugstores in Salida, and the local market could not support that many. Consequently, Alexander bought out Leonard R. Maier; his arrangement was that he would take the stock, while another druggist, Conrad Waggener, would take the fixtures.

By 1913, Alexander—with the best financial rating of all the Salida jewelers—found time to go into politics. He served three terms as mayor of Salida: 1913–15, 1915–17 and 1927–29. In 1926, he became chairman of the Republican County Central Committee and served until his death. He was president of the Colorado Pharmacal Association and twice elected president of the Salida Chamber of Commerce. And he seemingly rose to high office in most fraternal organizations he joined: Worthy Grand Patron of the Grand Chapter of Colorado, Order of the Eastern Star; Worshipful Master, Salida Lodge A.F. & A.M.; and Exalted Ruler, Salida Lodge No. 808, B.P.O. Elks, and a district deputy of that organization.

In the 1930s, Alexander took up genealogy as a hobby, eventually joining the Sons of the American Revolution on the strength of his ancestors Andrew McCormick (died 1797), a private in the Continental army under General Nathanael Greene, and Captain Joseph Raeburn (1733–1799). He became so well informed about American history that he was "distinguished as an after dinner speaker, as a toastmaster, and as a host in his home," as the *Salida Daily* put it on October 10, 1941.

Alexander had been appointed to the Colorado State Board of Pharmacy by Governor Ralph Lawrence Carr and served as its president. On a visit to Denver to preside over a board meeting, he had a heart attack and died after two weeks on October 7, 1941, at St. Luke's Hospital there. Services were held in Salida two days later; a bodyguard of Masons accompanied the funeral procession, and the Colorado State Board of Pharmacy and the Colorado Pharmaceutical Association sent representatives. "Salida industry halted at 3 o'clock while hundreds of residents from every walk of life, and many visitors from neighboring towns, crowded the [Alexander] home and lawn to pay their last tribute to a distinguished fellow citizen," reported the *Salida Record* on October 10, 1941.

Harriet inherited the entire estate (the Alexanders had no children), including the business, their house, shares in a number of dividend-paying companies and a 1941 Nash sedan. Independently wealthy, like her husband she took an interest in civic affairs, becoming active in Republican politics and serving as president of the Republican Women's Club "for a number of years," according to her obituary in the *Salida Mail* on August 4, 1971. She was the first woman elected to the Salida Town Council and served from

1953 to 1963. The Salida airport was named for her in 1964. Harriet died on August 3, 1971, at the age of eighty-nine.

Despite Alexander's claim to Zerbe in 1918 that he had no Lesher Dollars on hand, in fact he had "several" squirreled away. According to the *Salida Mountain Mail* of April 30, 1969, Harriet sold them for five dollars each during the Depression to a collector in Denver, possibly Edward Broadbent Morgan, president of the State Historical and Natural History Society of Colorado. They must be all or part of the hoard of six pieces known to Dr. Whiteley, *still* squirreled away somewhere.

Harriet recounted an even stranger anecdote in this article: "A few years later [than the early 1930s] a miner in Mexico discovered one of the eight-sided Lesher dollars. He contacted Mr. Alexander offering to exchange the coin for a silver tie pin and the transaction was completed. Mrs. Alexander sold the coin to a second collector for $25 a few years after the death of her husband." This must be no. 2, listed by Wilde as having been sold by "Alexander" to Dr. Philip W. Whiteley; this is an error coin, with the reverse die rotated one-eighth to the right.

Chapter 16

Goodspeed & Co., Colorado Springs Jewelers

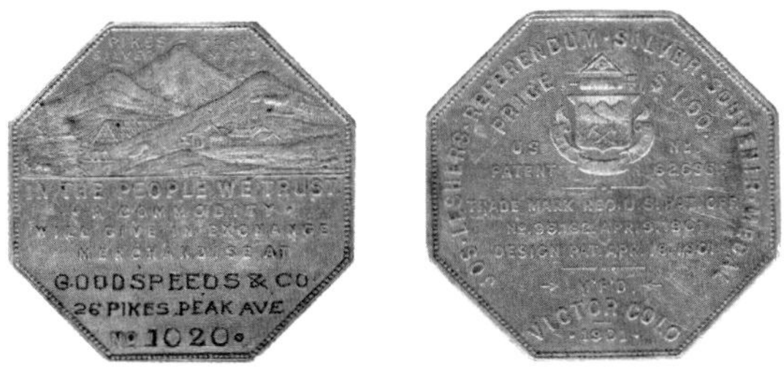

While Imprint-Type Lesher Dollars are known engraved (not stamped) GOODSPEEDS & CO/ 26 PIKES PEAK AVE, the correct business style was Goodspeed & Company, as shown in their advertising in 1901–2. Probably Lesher had them done in Victor by someone who was uncertain whether the correct business style was "Goodspeed's" or "Goodspeed & Co.," since the actual jeweler would not have made this mistake. And Mr. Goodspeed himself was not involved, he having died almost a decade earlier. Per Farran Zerbe, they had a few engraved to test demand for them, "expecting later to have some stamped," but this was not done. Only five are known today, of almost random numbers, though Wilde supposed that as many as fifteen might have been engraved based on the numbers known (27, 1014–27).

Lewis G. Goodspeed was born in Chicago, Illinois, on December 29, 1846, the son of Albert Griffith Goodspeed and his first wife, Abigail (Crane). From an old New England family, Lewis was ninth in descent from Roger Goodspeed, a co-founder or early proprietor of Barnstable, Massachusetts, founded in 1639. His father, educated in the Blendon Young Men's Seminary, Westerville, Ohio, married Abigail Crane of Delaware County, Ohio, on

Actual size, 32 mm. *Courtesy of Christopher Marchase.*

March 2, 1843. From this union four children were born, but two of Lewis's siblings died in infancy, and his mother followed when he was only twelve. His father moved to Illinois a year later and remarried.

When the census enumerator visited the Goodspeed farm at Waltham, La Salle County, Illinois, on July 15, 1860, Lewis was recorded as having attended school within the past year. But this is the last time he can be found in the U.S. Census, because he became a traveling agent for large "eastern" jewelry manufacturers after leaving school and spent much of his time on the road. Having "a very genial nature" (according to his obituary in the *Colorado Springs Weekly Telegraph* on August 13, 1892), he was quite successful.

About 1879, he moved to Chicago and opened a sales office at 149 State Street. While in town, he met twenty-three-year-old dressmaker Fannie Goetchins. Fannie's father had recently died in New Jersey, and her mother, Adelaide (Dobson) Goetchius [*sic*], and Fannie had moved in with Fannie's uncle, Edelbert Dobson, on Chicago's Near North Side. (The Dutch Goetchius family was indifferent as to the consistent spelling of their surname: Fannie used "Goetchins," while her younger brother Alfred Moser preferred "Goetchius" most of the time. Other variations are found in the census reports.)

Lewis and Fannie fell in love and were married in Chicago on Saturday, October 30, 1880. Where they resided the next few years is not known. By 1885, however, Lewis was living in the upscale Chicago suburb of Lake View (annexed to Chicago 1889), now with his mother-in-law and brother-in law, and was the owner of L.G. Goodspeed & Co., watch materials, 63 State Street. Brother-in-law Alfred was employed as a clerk at 125 State Street, fifth floor. The *1886 Chicago City Directory* showed that Lewis G. Goodspeed & Co. had moved to 125 State Street also, and Goodspeed had a partner, L.H. Guernsey (misspelled "Guerney" in the directory). As of 1887, Goodspeed was listed in the city directory as "watchmakers' tools."

Meanwhile, in the spring of 1880, Lucien C. Davis of Colorado Springs entered into a partnership in the jewelry business with T.J. Williams, according to the *Weekly Gazette* of April 10, 1880. (At this time, Colorado Springs was nothing like the huge city it is today; it was more a resort than a mining center. However, railroad service on the Denver and Rio Grande had begun in 1871.) By 1886, Davis was conducting a jewelry store at 15 South Tejon Street in downtown Colorado Springs, together with G.W. Davis, a young relative who shared his address. But on September 7, 1887, he died, leaving a widow; G.W. Davis took charge of the business. Mrs. L.C. Davis was probably anxious to wind up affairs.

How Goodspeed learned of this situation is not known. But late this year or early the next, he apparently sold out his Chicago interests, working for a time out of his old building as a commercial traveler. He probably moved to Colorado Springs in the spring of 1888. The *1888 Colorado Springs City Directory* listed him as a watchmaker and jeweler in the Davis store, with no address; most likely he stayed in the newly built Antlers Hotel nearby while he learned the business and considered an offer.

In early June, he concluded arrangements and purchased the Davis stock, as reported in the *Weekly Gazette* on June 16, 1888, becoming owner of the store and retaining "the services of Messrs. S.J. Pullin and Louis Langbehn, who have been connected with the establishment for some time. Both gentlemen are practical jewelers of long experience and the public will receive the same courteous treatment which has been accorded them in the past." He found a place to live, and Fannie joined him.

At about the same time, Goodspeed's former partner in the jewelers' supplies business, L.H. Guernsey, came to Colorado himself to direct the affairs of the C.H. Green Jewelry Co., established in Denver in March 1889. Alfred M. Goetchius—who must have known Guernsey from working as a jewelry clerk in the same building in Chicago for several years—was immediately hired as clerk, and his mother moved to Denver to live with him instead of with her daughter in Colorado Springs.

Goodspeed began "building up a fine business" in Colorado Springs, per his obituary. Before long, he moved around the corner, on the same block, to a better location at 26 East Pikes Peak Avenue. On June 3, 1890, he presented prizes at Colorado College to the best drilled cadets; each was a "handsome" gold medal "designed very appropriately for the occasion, with crossed muskets on a circle of gold," according to the *Colorado Springs Gazette*.

On February 6, 1891, Adelaide Goetchins, Goodspeed's mother-in-law, died, and she was buried in Riverside Cemetery, Denver, the next day.

In the summer of 1892, Fannie traveled to the East, ignorant of the fact that her husband had been exposed to typhoid fever. But he became ill, and toward the end of July, his symptoms increased in severity. She came back to nurse him about the beginning of August, to no avail; Lewis Goodspeed succumbed to typhoid on Monday, August 8, at ten o'clock in the morning, at age forty-seven. In Colorado Springs, he had owned L.G. Goodspeed, Watchmaker and Jeweler, just over four years. Fannie had his body shipped to Denver, and he is buried next to her mother in Riverside Cemetery.

Fannie was appointed administrator of Goodspeed's estate, but since she had had little involvement in the store, she called on her brother Alfred—

who had by now worked in the jewelry business about seven years—for help. He soon relocated to Colorado Springs from Denver, and an ad in the *Colorado Springs Gazette* on November 6, 1892, names him as "A.M. GOETCHINS, Manager."

The Goodspeed business prospered under Alfred's direction. An optical department was added by September 1894, and in January 1896, J.S. Brooker was hired to manage the manufacturing department. In February 1898, Alfred visited Chicago to purchase stock, representing himself as "managing the estate of the late L.G. Goodspeed and [conducting] the jewelry business there," per the *Western Supplement Jewelers Circular* of March 2, 1898. Goodspeed's was a frequent advertiser in the *Colorado Springs Gazette* in the 1890s and early 1900s.

The 1900 Lesher Dollar was mentioned in several stories in the *Colorado Springs Gazette*, and the *Denver Post* of May 3, 1901, reported that "the [Imprint-Type] Lesher referendum dollar is now in circulation." Noticing this, Alfred ordered a few samples engraved for him but apparently was dissatisfied with demand. They are not mentioned in his ads of the time.

After nearly a decade, he finally wound up the Goodspeed estate and settled with his sister: on April 30, 1902, Alfred Mosher Goetchius, in an affidavit of co-partnership, swore that "he is the sole owner of the Jewelry business carried on in Colorado Springs, El Paso County, Colorado, under the name of Goodspeed and Company." He became treasurer of the Colorado Springs Elks Club in April 1903 and continued to operate the business under the Goodspeed & Co. name for a time. But in April 1904, he sold it to Philip Zehner, a Goodspeed's employee "[f]or some time," who renamed it the Zehner Jewelry Co.

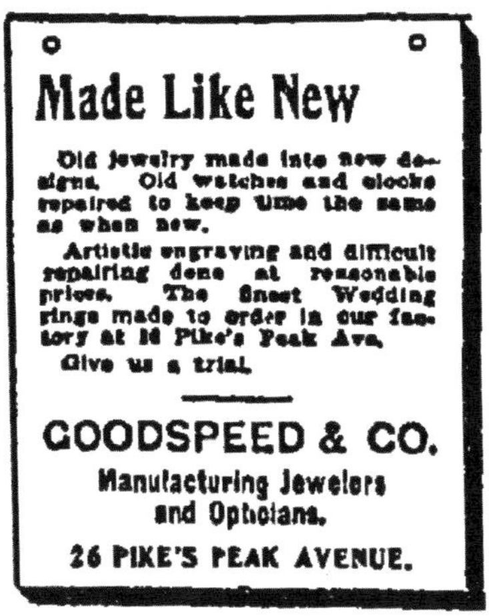

Goodspeed's ad in the *Colorado Springs Gazette*, May 1, 1901, 26 Pikes Peak Avenue.

Later that year, Alfred married thirty-two-year-old Cora Alice Gillette of Iowa. He continued to list himself in the Colorado Springs directory as a jeweler, as though he expected to work for others locally. This did not pan out; Alfred and Cora seem to have left town for a while, but by 1907 they were back, though Alfred had had to take a job as a clerk for the telephone company. Seeing no future there, he moved to Goldfield, Nevada, the next year but missed out on the boom; gold production in 1908 was down by almost half of that of 1907. The census of 1910 found him farther west still, working in Island County, Washington, as superintendent of a gold mine. He at last gained success as a poultry farmer in Island County, among other settlers of Dutch descent. Alfred died in Everett, Washington, on January 24, 1929, at age sixty. He is buried in Sunnyside Cemetery, Coupeville, Island County, Washington, next to Cora Alice, who followed him in death on November 11, 1932.

Fannie Goodspeed's life took a very different path; she became a social worker at "a rescue home for…destitute and erring girls and their children." After Lewis's death, she seems to have begun traveling, though she considered Colorado Springs her home; when she registered at the fancy Knutsford Hotel in Salt Lake City on February 11, 1897, she wrote that she was from Colorado Springs. Fannie liked Salt Lake City so much that she stayed there for a time, living in a boardinghouse. Evidently she had plenty of money from Goodspeed & Co.

It was not until 1907 that she definitely returned to Colorado Springs, where she appears in the directory at a boardinghouse. Fannie is missing from the 1908 directory but reappears in 1909 at a different boardinghouse. In that year or the next, however, she moved to Chicago to live with her younger sister Mary "May" Goetchins Bookwalter.

In 1863, the Seventh-day Adventist Church was formally organized, with headquarters in Battle Creek, Michigan. It emphasized evangelism, schools (including a medical college) and medical institutions, beginning with the Battle Creek sanitarium, founded in 1866. Missions to "skid row" people, prisoners and unwed mothers were soon begun. The church grew rapidly in the latter part of the nineteenth and early twentieth centuries. Colorado Springs had a Seventh-day Adventist church by 1903.

By 1910, Fannie was a Seventh-day Adventist; she became assistant matron at an Adventist home for girls in Chicago that year. Two years later, by then a "prominent social worker," she moved to Byron Center, Michigan (seven miles from Grand Rapids), to assume the position of assistant matron of the Michigan Home for Girls, founded in 1903 by William and Mary McKee on a farm there. But in August 1913, a severe heat wave in the Grand Rapids area resulted in the deaths of four young children and hastened hers also.

Fannie had been suffering from chronic Bright's disease (nephritis) for some time. She was found unresponsive in her room following the intense heat of Saturday night, August 16; her physician was called, but she died just before noon the next day without regaining consciousness. She was fifty-six.

Chapter 17

W.F. White, Grand Junction Department Store

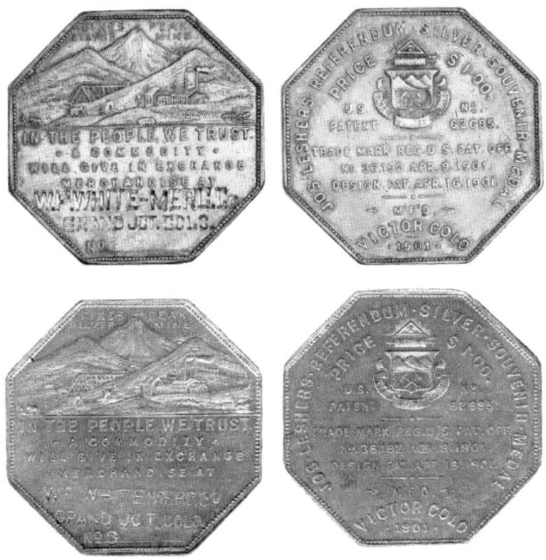

Imprint-Type Lesher Dollars are known stamped W.F. WHITE MERC. C°/ GRAND JCT. COLO. In 1914, Joseph Lesher remembered selling Lesher Dollars to a clothier in Grand Junction but could not then recall the name. He told Farran Zerbe that they had been supplied in blank, so White must have had them stamped locally.

At present eight are known, stamped with numbers from 1 to 36; Wilde estimated that fifty were ordered, which seems reasonable. Nearly all show signs of circulation: in 1969, Mrs. W.C. Alexander, then eighty-seven, recalled that "Lesher coins were used in Grand Junction," according to the *Salida Mountain Mail* of April 30, 1969.

The coins above are shown actual size, 32 mm. *Top row courtesy of American Numismatic Society, New York. Bottom row courtesy of Christopher Marchase.*

In addition to these is a ninth example, unnumbered but with the same text crudely engraved in tall, square letters. Its history can be learned from Farran Zerbe's post-1918 correspondence on Lesher Dollars, preserved in the archives of the American Numismatic Society, New York.

On October 3, 1932, Zerbe—then curator of the Chase National Bank Collection of Moneys of the World but still collecting Lesher Dollars privately—wrote to famous Fort Worth coin dealer B. Max Mehl, reporting that he had just obtained an example of J.E. Nelson's piece (chapter 11) and asking for information on any others unlisted in his 1918 article on the subject. He mentioned that Nelson and White were the only varieties discovered since then that he was aware of.

In response, Mehl wrote, "As you probably know, I have the [C.E.] Briggs Collection of Leshers to be sold in my next Sale. I found in it a White Lesher on which the imprint was faked." (Mehl held it back from the auction on November 8, 1932.) This was news to Zerbe, who asked for a full description, but Mehl put him off until he was "over the rush of the sale," adding, however, "regarding the WHITE Lesher, I feel sure there was one in the Mann Collection." But nothing more was heard of this coin until 1934.

In *The Numismatist* for May 1934, Chas. H. Fisher advertised that his next auction would feature a "Unique Lesher Dollar." Zerbe asked to examine it before the auction, and Fisher obliged; Zerbe was not impressed. "You should check up on this piece," Zerbe wrote to Fisher on June 20, 1934. "I believe that you will agree with me that the imprint is engraved, and in my judgment not a very good job at that. I have never inspected a W.F. White Lesher piece but from two sources I have been informed that there was a regularly stamped imprint specimen in the Mann Collection." This was correct; the collection of H.O. Mann of Denver (August 14, 1858–June 15, 1922) included two, nos. 3 and 36. Since the Imprint Type existed completely blank, Zerbe wrote, "We must be alert for fabrications of imprint." But he did not condemn it outright.

Concerned, Fisher wrote on June 26 to his consigner, C.E. Briggs, who had received the White piece back from Mehl in 1932 when it was rejected as a fake. Fisher mentioned that he had not indicated that Briggs was the consigner but asked, "Can you give me something of its history?...This might be a fabrication."

Briggs responded with a scrawled handwritten letter dated July 2:

> *In regard to the Lesher all I can say is a friend of mine gave me this piece to sell for her* [in 1932, apparently] *with the understanding that I was not*

> *to tell anyone where I got it. She says it is the same as the one in the Mann Col. and guarantees it to be so. As to the imprint being engraved I saw the Mann Piece once years ago and my recollection is that that one is ingraved* [sic].... *What I mean by the same is The imprint words and Name and spelling all the same and must have been done by the same party that did the Mann Piece.*

Apparently, Fisher shared this curious guarantee with Zerbe, for it is found among his correspondence. Mollified by this incorrect authentication—for the Mann pieces are stamped, not engraved—Zerbe bought it at Fisher's auction on August 23, 1934. He exhibited it at the October 12, 1934 meeting of the New York Numismatic Club and donated it on December 10, 1947, with the rest of his second Lesher Dollar collection, to the American Numismatic Society, where it remains.

But who was the mystery woman who asked Briggs to sell it for her secretly? The wife of an impecunious or senile collector? Or a fraudster, passing off a crude fake as the real thing? The authors are inclined to view this piece as a pattern made by White to see how his intended lettering would look before he had a stamp made, simply because it is so different from the stamped pieces—and because it lacks a number, which would be easier to add than all this text. But we may never know.

As for the issuer, William Foster White's parents, Matthew C. and Martha J., were born in Kentucky and later moved to Stockton, Missouri, where William was born on June 26, 1859. Matthew was a successful master carpenter. William attended school there.

Like many other Lesher Dollar issuers, he had a varied career after leaving school. "At the age of 14 years he learned telegraphy, which he followed for a number of years," according to his obituary in the *Grand Junction Daily Sentinel* of February 6, 1911. He began working for the Missouri Pacific Railroad (later renamed the Missouri, Kansas and Texas) and rose to the post of station agent at Muskogee, Indian Territory, by 1880. (In his obituary, he was said to have been "chief dispatcher and division superintendent of the Missouri, Kansas & Texas Railroad at Muskogee, I.T. for a time," which described his duties but not his title.) White was a diligent worker there, and the reporter for the *Muskogee Indian Journal* found him to be "genial."

But his promising career in the railroad industry came to an abrupt end in 1881, when "during a fuss between station-agent White and Jack Badger, yard-master here, Badger called White a liar, and when requested to take it back, refused, when White promptly downed him with a paper weight." White resigned the same day, effective November 1. (Both stories appeared in the same issue of the *Indian Journal*, October 13, 1881.)

Out of railroading for good, White drifted around for a year or so. He returned to Missouri and worked briefly as a drugstore clerk for friends or relatives in Pilot Grove and Appleton. He took a course at the Sedalia Business College, perhaps in the summer of 1882, when he seems to have been living with his older married sister, Edith Murphy, according to the *Sedalia Weekly Bazoo* of July 11, 1882. White then settled on a career in pharmacy, conducting a drugstore in the southern Colorado coal mining boomtown of Walsenburg for about seven years.

While there, he made the acquaintance of another twenty-something businessman, Charles E. Mitchell. Mitchell had come to Colorado in 1880 as "one of a party sent out by the government to survey the Ute Indian reservation for the first time," according to his obituary in the *Routt County (CO) Sentinel* on June 10, 1910. (Most of the Indians were later forcibly removed to Utah, though the Southern Ute Indian Reservation remains in southwestern Colorado.)

Mitchell settled in Grand Junction, Colorado, which became open to settlement on September 4, 1881, and received that name on November 5, 1882. But he did not remain a surveyor; he opened a drugstore there (the requirements for becoming a pharmacist were obviously very loose in the West in the 1880s). Grand Junction was the seat of Mesa County and an agricultural center.

In October 1889, these two Colorado druggists formed a partnership in Grand Junction, White & Mitchell—but for the hardware business, not drugs. The thrifty White soon felt secure enough to marry, and he wed Frances "Fannie" Phillips, twenty-two, of Jackson County, Missouri, in Kansas City on September 28, 1892. Following his marriage, White acquired an interest in a state bank in Deepwater, Missouri, becoming cashier "for some time," according to his obituary in the *Daily Sentinel*.

The hardware business prospered, and White bought out his partner's interest in 1895, operating as the W.F. White Hardware Co. Mitchell moved to Aspen to "[engage] in the pharmacy business," per Mitchell's obituary. A daughter, Vivian, was born to William and Fannie on September 8, 1895.

Until 1899, White evidently followed the usual practice of rural merchants of selling on credit. But on February 17, 1899, he began advertising a "new system, SELLING FOR CASH AT REDUCED PRICES," which he said "is proving a greater success than we anticipated." By the end of 1900, the

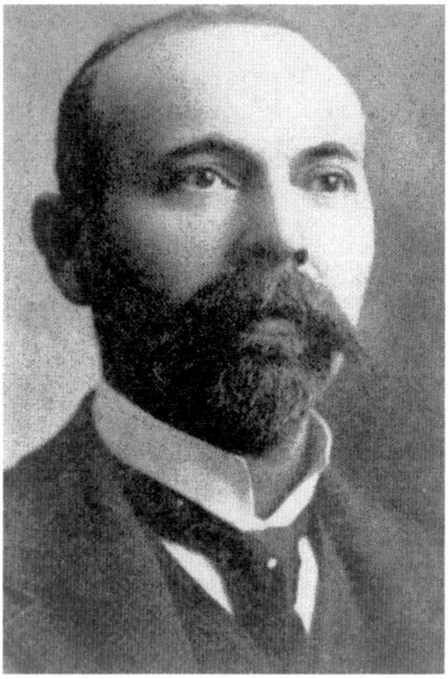

Left: W.F. White as trustee of Grand Junction Elk Lodge, No. 575, 1900. *Priscilla Mangnall,* Grand Junction Museum: Our First 50 Years 1900–1950, Lodge 575, Benevolent and Protective Order of Elks *(Grand Junction, CO, 1950).*

Below: W.F. White Mercantile Co. ad. *R.L. Polk & Co.'s Grand Junction City Directory*, 1902.

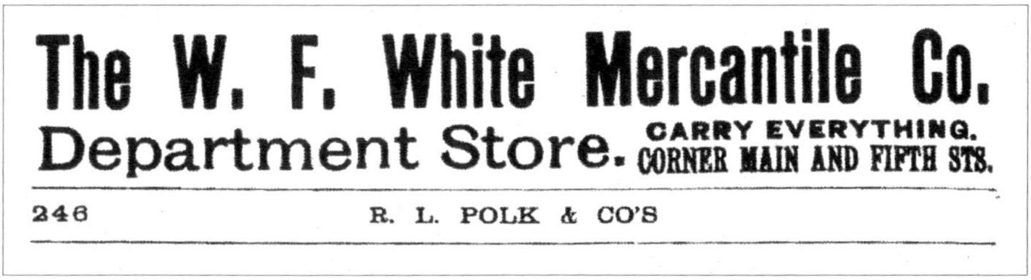

White Hardware Company had expanded far beyond hardware into shoes and jewelry, as seen by its newspaper ad of December 31, 1900. White recognized this, probably during 1901, by renaming the business "The W.F. White Mercantile Co. Department Store" in time to advertise his new name in the Grand Junction city directory for 1902. He continued to expand into soft goods, and the U.S. Census taken in April 1910 gives his occupation as "clothing store."

But White began to show symptoms of tuberculosis after the turn of the century and was forced to decline an appointment by Governor John J. Shafroth (1909–13) "soon after because of his poor health." On June 21, 1910, he sold the W.H. White Mercantile Co. to the Union Trading Co. (a branch of the Farmers' Union association) for $35,000, giving immediate possession. (In less than two years, the Union Trading Co. was bankrupt.) But White's health continued to decline, and he succumbed on February 5, 1911, in Grand Junction. He was buried in Elmwood Cemetery, Kansas

City, Missouri; Fannie was laid to rest next to him there after her death on September 27, 1936.

A Free Silver man, White was active in Democratic politics. "He was a delegate to every democratic state convention as long as his health permitted," per his obituary. After Charles S. Thomas, a Democrat, took office as governor of Colorado in 1899, he gave White a commission as colonel on his staff on April 1, 1899, and White styled himself Colonel White ever after. In Grand Junction, "Colonel White was also one of the incorporators of the old electric-light company. He was a faithful member of the local lodge of Elks."

After his death, White was recalled fondly: "As a business man he had the respect of everyone who had dealings with him, and his reputation for honesty and integrity might be envied by anyone. His competitors found him a square man of honor, and his friends bear witness to his generous nature and warm-heartedness to those in need of counsel or material aid."

Chapter 18

The Uniques

A.W. Clark, H.H. Rosser and H. Stein

These men were not agents or issuers but simply persons who had their names engraved on blank Imprint-Type dollars as a presentation piece or keepsake. Dr. Whiteley wrote that they were "Unknown to Zerbe," but this is not so at least in the case of Clark.

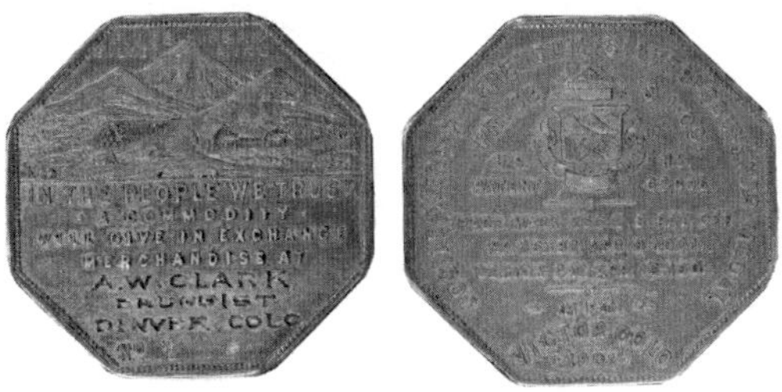

A.W. Clark

A.W. Clark, a druggist in Denver, had an Imprint dollar engraved A.W. CLARK/ DRUGGIST/ DENVER, COLO. When this piece surfaced in 1998, it was described in *Numismatic News*, December 22, 1998, as "previously unreported." However, it was in fact shown to Farran Zerbe in 1921 and is

Actual size, 32 mm. *Courtesy of Brad Rodgers.*

recorded in his unpublished second edition of *Private Silver Coins Issued in the United States: The Leshers or Referendum Pieces*, November 9, 1934 (corrected typescript preserved in the archives of the American Numismatic Society, New York). Zerbe wrote, "A variety which may some day be claimed of good standing is [description]. This piece, which is numbered 1, was engraved for Mr. Clark about 1917 especially to present to his friend Mr. C.W. Cowell as a token of many years friendship."

Thus, it was not made until long after Lesher Dollars ceased to circulate and is a presentation piece to Charles W. Cowell of Denver (August 1841–December 15, 1921), one of the most active Lesher Dollar collectors of the day.

Alfred W. Clark, the issuer (August 31, 1860–January 25, 1924), "conducted a retail drug store on Santa Fe Avenue in Denver," per Tom Hallenbeck in the *Numismatic News* article, from 1889 until his death. How Clark became acquainted with Mr. Cowell is not known; apparently he was not a coin collector.

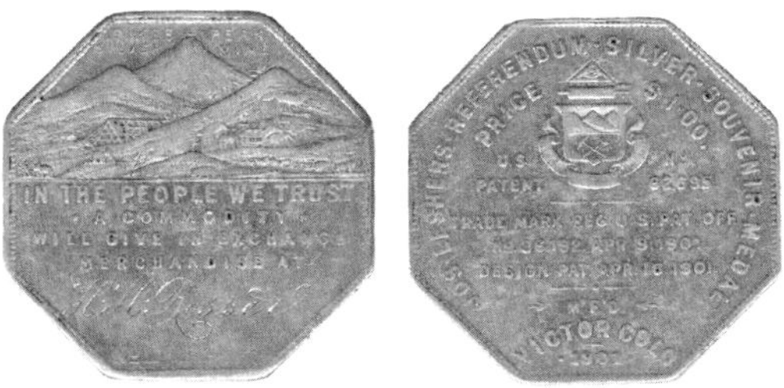

H.H. ROSSER

A 1901 Imprint Dollar exists engraved "H.H. Rosser" in script, without a number. Though no business or location is mentioned, this is known to have been issued by Henry Hopkins Rosser (August 1869–December 26, 1941), proprietor of a cigar store in Victor, Colorado (1901–41). Formerly a druggist in Coal Creek, Colorado, Rosser moved to bustling Victor to switch

Actual size, 32 mm. *Courtesy of Christopher Marchase.*

to stationery, cigars and confectionery, soon adding a billiard room. After his death, a relative found this piece in his store.

Rosser likely had it made as a souvenir of his new venture in Victor, buying it from Sam Cohen or even Lesher himself, since it is unnumbered. A Democrat, he served as county chairman for Teller County for a time.

Although Whiteley did not reveal that he owned this piece until 1955, in a paper ("Colorado Specie") read before the American Numismatic Association convention educational panel, he may have acquired it directly from the estate; he was collecting Lesher Dollars in 1941 and read a paper on them to the Denver Coin Club early that year.

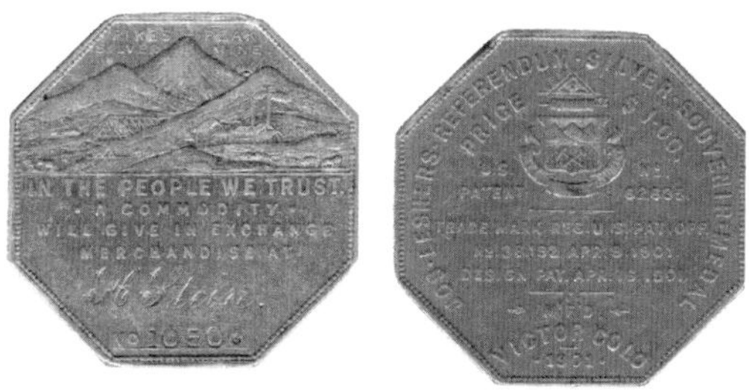

H. Stein

A similar Imprint Dollar engraved "H. Stein." in script (in a different hand than H.H. Rosser), with no. 1050 punched in, appeared as lot 2986 of the August 16–21, 1952 ANA Convention Sale Catalogue, the last coin in a consignment of fifty-three mixed Lesher Dollars by O.K. Rumbel of Mission, Texas. Cataloger John J. Ford, Jr. wrote, "It is believed that Mr. Stein was a Clothier in Canon City, Colo., but this information cannot be verified." Apparently this is derived from Zerbe, 1918, page 164: "Others said to have purchased Leshers for trade use were…two clothiers, Lesher says probably at Canon City and Grand Junction, Colo." On this slender thread hangs the attribution of the H. Stein piece to Canon City, Colorado.

Actual size, 32 mm. *Courtesy of Christopher Marchase.*

In February 1978, Adna G. Wilde, Jr. wrote that his research had "revealed that Mr. Stein was a printer in Canon City, Colorado." However, in 1995, Robert Kincaid and Sandra Slater engaged Carol and John Fox, and they reported that they "researched the Canon City directories from 1901 to 1910. Only Stein mentioned was Jesus Stein [whose] occupation was laborer." Thus, "H. Stein" was neither a clothier nor a printer in Canon City circa 1901.

In Dr. Whiteley's 1955 paper, reprinted in *The Numismatist*, July 1958, page 790, he wrote, "There were two prominent men in Denver, circa 1920–21, who collected Lesher pieces [Charles W. Cowell and H.O. Mann]....These two collectors competed with one another for Leshers. My Leshers were obtained from one source [Mann] and the name and address of the prior owner of the rare ones is in my possession. I am intimating that the other source may have secured some blank imprints and created a few varieties."

O.K. Rumbel purchased this coin at the 126th Auction Sale of M.H. Bolender, September 23, 1939, lot 1387, consigner unknown. But it was attributed as Zerbe 5 (i.e., the cataloguer attached no significance to the engraved name) and was the only Lesher Dollar in the sale. While Whiteley was not wrong about Cowell (see A.W. Clark), the H. Stein piece cannot have any connection to Mann.

However, Kincaid and Slater *did* find a Henry Stein (1847–1907), a soft drink bottler in Florence, Colorado—though he had the wrong occupation and residence. But see chapter 13; Lesher had an "exclusive agent" in Florence, C.W. Thomas, who sold his pieces blank. Perhaps Henry Stein bought one from him as a souvenir, asking for his name to be engraved on it. But unless new information becomes available, this attribution is speculative.

Bibliography

The principal references for Lesher Dollars utilizing original sources are:

Adams, Edgar H. "The Lesher Referendum Dollar." *The Numismatist* 24, no. 8 (August 1911): 270–71.

Briggs, Charles E. "The Lesher Coins." *The Numismatist* 33, no. 12 (December 1920): 546–48.

"The Career of Joseph Lesher." *The Numismatist* 34, no. 4 (April 1921): 150–51.

Cohen, Sam L. *Gold Rush De Luxe*. New York: Sam L. Cohen, 1940, 40–43.

[Ford, John J., Jr.]. *1952 A.N.A. Convention Sale Catalog*. New York: New Netherlands Coin Co., Inc., 1952: 112–15.

Hibler, Harold E., and Charles V. Kappan. *So-Called Dollars*. New York: Coin and Currency Institute, Inc., 1963. [No original research; derived from Zerbe, Ford and Whiteley. However, Hibler and Kappan included Lesher Dollars as part of a series of dollar-size medals, assigning new HK numbers (in an irregular manner), which are used by some grading services in preference to Zerbe numbers.]

Rochette, Ed. "The Ghost of Joseph Lesher." *The Numismatist* 97, no. 11 (November 1984): 2337–40. [Note: Rochette was misinformed as to the "Miller Badge and Button Company" striking Lesher Dollars; his informant confused Frank F. Hurd with Isadore Miller, whose company did not exist in 1900–1. The actual maker is unknown.]

Slater, Sandra Gray. "John Nelson and the Nebraska Lesher Dollar." *The Numismatist* 110, no. 4 (April 1997): 387–91.

Stowers, Charles A. "The Riddle of the Nebraska Lesher." *The Numismatist* 100, no. 1 (January 1991): 64–67.

Whiteley, Dr. Philip W. "Colorado Specie." *The Numismatist* 71, no. 7 (July 1958): 783–91 (reprint of a paper read before the American Numismatic Association convention educational panel, 1955).

———. "The Lesher Story." *The Numismatic Scrapbook Magazine* 24 (1958): 2047–53, 2328–35 and 2829–38; reprinted n.d., n.p. (Chicago).

Wilde, Adna G., Jr. "Lesher Referendum Medals: Where Are They Today?" *The Numismatist* 91, no. 2 (February 1978): 229–48.

Zerbe, Farran. "Private Silver Coins Issued in the United States: The Leshers or Referendum Pieces." *American Journal of Numismatics* 51 (1918): 152–66.

———. Revised edition (unpublished corrected typescript in archives of American Numismatic Society, New York), November 9, 1934.

About the Authors

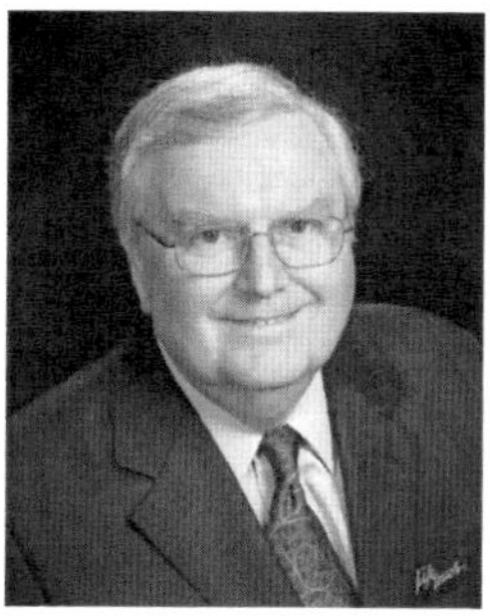

Robert D. Leonard Jr.

Bob Leonard, a fellow of the American Numismatic Society, New York, has studied private coinages, including Lesher Dollars, since the 1960s. Author of over one hundred numismatic articles and lead author of *California Pioneer Fractional Gold: Historic Gold Rush Small Change 1852–1857* and *Suppressed Jewelers' Issues 1858–1882 by Walter Breen and Ronald J. Gillio*, Second Ed., this is his third book. He examined the pertinent Secret Service records in the National Archives and Farran Zerbe's papers in the archives of the American Numismatic Society, in addition to verifying and expanding the genealogical research presented here.

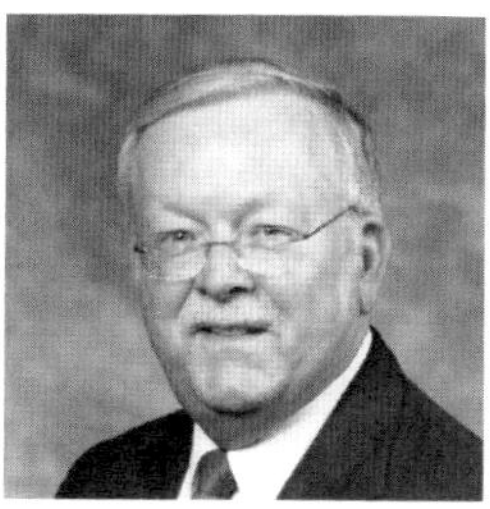

Kenneth L. Hallenbeck

A former insurance executive, Ken Hallenbeck moved to Colorado Springs in 1977 to assume the post of curator of the museum of the American Numismatic Association, leaving in 1983 to found Ken Hallenbeck Coin Gallery Inc. there. He has held other positions with the ANA, including president (1989–91) and acting executive director, and is a former director of the Colorado Springs Pioneer Museum Foundation. He has been studying and dealing in Lesher Dollars since the 1970s.

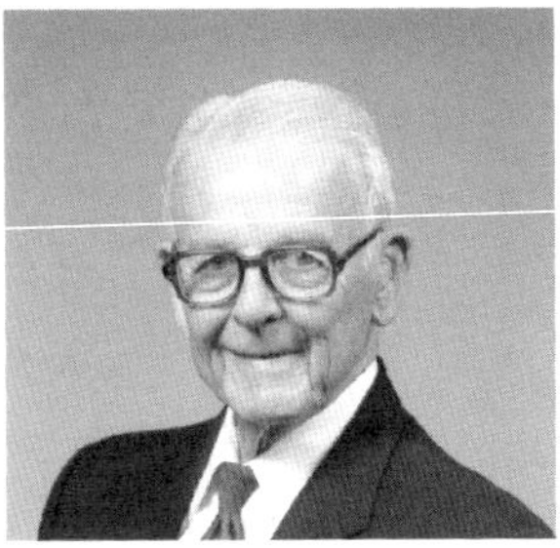

ADNA G. WILDE, JR.†
(OCTOBER 1, 1920–NOVEMBER 17, 2008)
A graduate of The Citadel, Colonel Wilde had a distinguished military career from 1943 to 1968, serving in Italy, Korea and Vietnam. He began collecting coins in 1947; held elective office in the American Numismatic Association, including president (1981–83); and was inducted into the ANA Numismatic Hall of Fame in 2002. A longtime student of Lesher Referendum Dollars, his groundbreaking study, "Lesher Referendum Medals: Where Are They Today?" (*The Numismatist*, February 1978), received the First Place Heath Literary Award and is essential for the understanding of these issues.